Is There An Islamic Problem?

Essays on Islamicate Societies, the US and Israel

M. SHAHID ALAM

The Other Press
Kuala Lumpur
2004

ISBN 983-9541-43-9

PUBLISHED 2004 BY
The Other Press
607 Mutiara Majestic
Jalan Othman
46000 Petaling Jaya
Selangor, Malaysia

WEBSITE
www.ibtbooks.com

COVER DESIGN BY
Habibur Rahman
bouncegraphics@yahoo.com

PRINTED BY
Academe Art and Printing Services
Kuala Lumpur

2004

Is There An Islamic Problem?

This book is dedicated to
all the victims of Empire,
who die and are maimed by the thousands
every day of the year
including September 11

"For each We have appointed a divine law and a traced-out way. Had Allah willed He could have made you one community. But that He may try you by that which He hath given you (He hath made you as ye are). So vie with one another in good works. Unto Allah will ye return, and He will then inform you of that wherein ye differ."

Qur'ān: 5:48

"O ye, who believe! Be ye staunch in justice, witnesses for Allah, even though it be against yourselves or (your) parents or (your) kindred, or whether (the case be of) a rich man or a poor man, for Allah is nearer unto both (than ye are)."

Qur'ān: 4: 135

Contents

Preface

"O David! Lo! We have set thee as a viceroy in the earth; therefore judge aright between mankind, and follow not desire that it beguile thee from the way of Allah. Lo! those who wander from the way of Allah have an awful doom, forasmuch as they forgot the Day of Reckoning."

Qur'ān: 38: 26[1]

May 20, 2004

I have brought together in this book some of the essays I wrote after September 11, 2001, essays in which I have tried to make sense – historical sense – of the events which transpired on the morning of that fateful day, between 8:45 AM and 9:43 AM, when three hijacked airliners, converted into missiles, crashed into the Twin Towers and the Pentagon, killing 2752 people.[2]

Articulating their fear and dread, many Americans felt that the attacks of 9-11 had "changed the world forever." In large measure,

---

1 *The Glorious Qur'ān: Arabic Text and English Rendering, Text and Explanatory Translation by* Mohammad M. Pickthall (Des Plaines, IL.: Library of Islam, 1994). All Qur'ānic references are to this translation.

2 Phil Hirschkorn, "New York Reduced 9/11 Death Toll by 40," October 29, 2003: http://www.cnn.com/2003/US/Northeast/10/29/wtc.deaths/

this was true. Most Americans had never known what it felt to be victims; they had never lived in fear of attacks, from bombs, missiles and artillery shells. Only Americans had the right to deliver destruction to others; only they had the power to do this to anyone, at any time. Now, for the first time, death and destruction had been delivered to two iconic addresses in America. This was not expected. It was unfair. It was unnerving.

There are few moments in history, few horrors, that crystallize the contradictions of the reigning capitalist paradigm – contradictions that are concealed, papered over by the ideologues of that paradigm – the way that the attacks of 9-11 have done. I am referring here to the symbolism of these attacks. In the icons they attacked, no less than the deaths they inflicted or the methods they chose to deliver their message, the nineteen Arab men had put America on notice. This was the beginning of the third Islamicate riposte, several decades in the making, to the Western onslaughts against the Islamicate world that began in the late eighteenth century. The United States has the power to control the Islamicate states, but it appears now that both of them are under attack from Islamic peoples.

Only a few years back, Francis Fukuyama had announced to the world that man had finally reached the 'end of history,' that Hegel's Zeitgeist, after successively wrestling and defeating the fascist and communist challenges to freedom, had delivered history into the long-awaited Valhalla of liberal capitalism. The American model, combining free markets and democracy, had triumphed.[3] There might be a few road bumps ahead, but henceforth, it would be a straight and narrow path, paved with peace, prosperity, and, not to forget, unchallenged American supremacy.

---

[3] Francis Fukuyama, "The End of History?" *The National Interest*, (Summer 1989): 3-18. This was later written up into a book, *The End of History and the Last Man* (London: Hamish Hamilton, 1992).

Perhaps, the attacks of September 11 have ended this end-of-history fantasy. At least, some oracles are now proclaiming that history could not be sent into retirement; not just yet. Sorry, there is one more dragon to slay. A new fascism has reared its ugly head. It is fascism in its Islamic variant. Saint George must again sharpen his lance to slay the Islamic dragon. Why this unseemly retreat from a triumph that seemed complete just a few years back?

The attacks of September 11 are like an eruption, a volcanic eruption that has thrust lava and ashes from our netherworld, the dark netherworld of the Periphery, into the rich and tranquil landscape of America. In the past, we had succeeded in containing these eruptions *inside* the Periphery. The attacks of September 11 speak of a massive failure in a paradigm that has worked for two hundred years to keep the Periphery in its place, to contain the resistance against the Core within the bounds of the Periphery.

At first, and for the longest period, the Core kept the Periphery in check through colonization: through massacres, ethnic cleansings, concentration camps, apartheid and racism. Wc sent our men into the Periphery to do the job, telling them that they were on a civilizing mission; they were bringing good governance to the savages. We could always find natives to collaborate with us against their own kin and class. In time, the natives understood the game; they understood that they only labored for our profit. Taking advantage of our squabbles, the Periphery broke lose, starting in the 1940s.

This setback was temporary. In large part, the system managed to restore the *status quo ex ante.* Steadily, inevitably, Core capital took over the capital in the Periphery or bound it in a hundred ties of clientage, in unalterable relations of dependence. The Periphery was now run by native thugs who were our men. We armed them, trained them, provided them with intelligence, and, when they misbehaved, we knew how to get rid of them. The CIA took care of that.

When the Soviet Union collapsed in 1991, the Core was free, as it had never been before, to impose global rules that best served its corporate interests. Henceforth, all capital would be privatized; capital, goods and services would be free to move across all borders; indigenous capital in the Periphery would receive no preferences; and property rights in intellectual capital would be strengthened. In 1994, the World Trade Organization (WTO) was created to join the IMF and World Bank in imposing these rules on the Periphery.

Once this new framework was in place, the Core encouraged elections everywhere, barring the Arab world. Democracy in the Periphery was now functional. It gave a measure of legitimacy to the branch-plant governments in the Periphery while ensuring that they would have no real power to challenge Core capital. Core capital never had a better deal. This was Valhalla.

Why did September 11 disturb the bliss of this Valhalla?

Directly and indirectly, the essays in this book provide answers to this question. September 11 brings into the open, forcing into the daylight of consciousness, the legacies of history – of racial hubris, of disequilibria imposed by wars, of messianism, of reincarnated fossils, of tribalism sanctified by religion, of social science in the service of power, of naked greed disguised in the rhetoric of the civilizing mission, of citizens fed on lies and sedated by amusements, of cruelty cultivated as a racial virtue, of injustices that cannot be allowed to stand. September 11 establishes beyond reasonable doubt that the United States is deeply, irrevocably connected to the Arab world, the Islamicate world, in ways it cannot ignore or deny. These essays map out the connections.

Notwithstanding its horror, September 11 was a symbol that spoke unmistakably of the manifold connections that tie the United States – through Zionism, through its messianism, through its links to an older past, through wars, through sanctions, through tens of billion of dollars in military aid, through coups, through partnerships with corrupt monarchies, through vetoes at the Security Council, through demonization of Islam, through the brothels of corporate media – to Palestinians, to Iraqis, to the Arab world, to the Islamicate world, to Africa, Asia and Latin America: in a word, to the Periphery. September 11 was a souvenir from the dark dungeons of our secret history, a digitized, televised image from the lost and forgotten Abu Ghraibs of decades past.

The symbolic power of 9-11 had to be suppressed. Instantly, the President, followed by the brothels of corporate media and the ideologues who pimp for authority, was spinning a thick web of lies and obfuscations around 9-11. The hijackers were emissaries *from* an evil place, a demon world, whose inhabitants worship false idols, and in daily rituals of blood sacrifices imprecate our democracy, our freedoms, our rights, our traditions of infinite justice. These devils hate us because we are so good, so virtuous, and so Christian.

September 11 was also welcomed by some in Israel and America. Yes, it was welcomed. The words are unmistakable. In an interview he gave to the *New York* Times, Benjamin Netanyahu, former Prime Minister of Israel, said the attacks are "very good" for relations between the United States and Israel.[4] The attacks were also very good for the neoconservatives, many of them friends of Israel, who were waiting for a "galvanizing event" to launch

4 James Bennet, "Spilled Blood Is Seen as Bond That Draws 2 Nations Closer," *New York Times* (September 12, 2001), section A, p. 22. col. 5.

their *Project for a New American Century*, which would make American power unchallengeable.[5] September 11 was their dream come true. In April 2003, they succeeded in leveraging 9-11 into an invasion of Iraq. That is now history. A few of the essays in this book are about this war too, its lies, its language, its links to the past, and its bitter legacy rapidly, unexpectedly unfolding before our eyes.

In gathering these essays, I am led to recall the support and friendship I rcccived along the way, as I looked for publishing outlets, and as I faced the wrath of cliques who have long sought to censor – too often successfully – any references to the crimes of their favorite tribe. I owe my deepest thanks to the two bold and doughty editors of *Counterpunch*, Jeffrey St. Claire and Alexander Cockburn, who first launched these essays, giving me the audience that the censors in mainstream media were determined to deny me. *Counterpunch* is one of the few points of light in a media space that is dominated by black holes.

I had few friends at Northeastern University before 9-11. I have fewer now. Only one colleague, Frank Naarendorp, professor of Psychology, stood by my side during my travails with people who wanted me fired from my job. I lost one friend when he discovered, on the eve of America's invasion of Iraq, that I was deficient in the measure of patriotism that translates into automatic support for *all* American wars, once they have been launched. I lost a second friend when I signed my name to the petition calling for the academic boycott of Israel. Israel can do nothing to deserve our moral censure, unless we also censure its victims in equal measure. Still, I remain

---

5 David Fitts, "Those Who Don't Remember History," *Ace Weekly* (April 10, 2003): www.aceweekly.com/Backissues_ACEWeekly/2003/030410/cover_story 030410. html

grateful to Northeastern University for tolerating my free speech – for leaving me alone – at a time when many outside and a few inside Northeastern sought my dismissal for exercising that right in ways that they found disagreeable.

Judging from their comments evaluating my courses, I like to think that my students are better disposed towards my critiques of global capitalism and the ideologies that support it. An occasional student will demand that I love it or leave it. Many more are more appreciative; a few even claim that they have been transformed. But I suspect that their appreciation probably has a short shelf-life.

Among my friends, Paul de Rooij receives my warmest gratitude. Paul is an economist based in London, who, at about the same time as I, decided to enter the public discourse, impelled I think by the same events that had moved me. Paul has long been an indefatigable advocate of the Palestinians in their struggle against Israeli Occupation. Though divided by an ocean, with a little help from the internet, over the past two years Paul has been a comrade in arms, an invaluable resource, occasionally a demanding editor, but always a delightful companion.

Many friends and fellow travelers offered hope, encouragement and friendship when others proffered insults, invectives and intimidations. In particular, I would like to acknowledge with gratitude the many kindnesses I have received from Ahrar Ahmad, Mumtaz Ahmed, Mohammed Aleem, Abdul Cader Asmal, Rauf Azhar, Mona Baker, Ken Barney, Belal Baquie, Shelagh Bocoum, Ashfak Bokhari, Zeljko Cipris, Hamid Dabashi, Lawrence Davidson, Sundeep Dougal, John Esposito, Ahmad Faruqui, Ted Honderich, Rashid Khalidi, Anwar Shahid Khan, Sarosh Khan, Rich LaRock, Aftab Malik, Muneeb Malik, Mustansir Mir, Enver Masud, Parviz Mirbaghi, Sheila Musaji, Ahmed Nassef, Marghoob Quraishi, Salim

Rashid, Syed Shakeel, Sunil Sharma, Lille Singh, George Saliba, Teepu Siddique, Denis Sullivan, Gale Toensing, Pankaj Topiwala and Asad Zaman. Some of them are old friends; some new; some I have not met but hope to meet soon.

My final acknowledgement is paternal. It goes to my son, Junaid, from whom I have learnt far more than he has from me, at least in the years during which he was negotiating his rites of passage. Instead of writing poetry, as I did to ease my passage, he was reading Karl Marx and Leon Trotsky. I think it all started when a teacher gave him a copy of Fanon's *The Wretched of the Earth*. I may have helped it along by giving him access to my copy of Aimé Césaire. I have since been wondering about whatever happened to all my talk about Rumi and the contemplative life. Was it only talk?

I hope that these essays will bear witness, faint witness though it is, that I have endeavored to be true to my *Rabb*, the single Lord of all Creation, to whom belong the most beautiful names, and, conversely, that I have labored to reject the false deities of tribe and cult, of racism and bigotry, because He, who is *Rahman* and *Raheem*, created us "from a single soul and from it created its mate, and from them twain hath spread abroad a multitude of men and women."[6] As a Muslim, to believe is to bear witness to our single humanity: our creation from, and connection to, a single soul.

"Our Lord! Cause not our hearts to stray after Thou hast guided us, and bestow upon us mercy from Thy Presence. Lo! Thou, only Thou art the Bestower."[7]

6 Qur'ān: 4:1.
7 Qur'ān: 3:8.

PART ONE

Islamicate Societies and the West

CHAPTER ONE

Is There an Islamic Problem?

"Thus We have appointed you a Middle Nation, that ye may be witnesses against mankind, and that the Messenger may be a witness against you."

Qur'ān: 2:143[1]

January 2, 2002

It has become fashionable after September 11, 2001, to excoriate Islam – the religion and civilization – as the source of the problems facing the Muslims. The air is thick with theories that identify Islam as the single greatest obstacle to the modernization of Islamicate societies. Oddly, after derailing modernization, that same Islam now fuels the rage over the absence of modernity in Islamicate societies.

In a recent essay, Pervez Hoodbhoy, a physicist and activist from Pakistan, argues that a deadening obscurantism has paralyzed Islamicate civilization since the twelfth century. Muslims can end this sustained paralysis, he writes, only if they decide to replace Islam

---

1 *The Glorious Qur'ān: Arabic Text and English Rendering, Text and Explanatory Translation by* Mohammad M. Pickthall (Des Plaines, IL.: Library of Islam, 1994). All quotes from the Qur'ān refer to this translation.

with secular humanism.[2] Perhaps unknowingly, Hoodbhoy echoes a common Orientalist fallacy, which speaks of an early decline in the vitality of Islamicate civilization. It is fitting that we take a closer look at this thesis and see if we can quickly lay it to rest.

There is a touching irony in Hoodbhoy's thesis – not intended by him, I think. He concludes, a bit pompously, that secular humanism "*alone* offers the hope of providing everybody on this globe with the right to life, liberty and the pursuit of happiness (emphasis added)." Hoodbhoy's faith is touching. It is also a bit ironic, given that he opens his essay by acknowledging that the United States – as he puts it, the "Grand Exorcist" – is busy pursuing its own "happiness" by "exacting blood revenge" for September 11. In blatant disregard of its founding principles, the Grand Exorcist has for decades – two hundred years, in the Western hemisphere – worked feverishly to deny basic human rights to more than three-fourths of humanity.

No doubt, there are Americans who cringe at actions of their government that undermine freedoms abroad. Sadly, they are too few to have made much difference. The only imperialist war that an American public has opposed was the Vietnam War, but that was mostly because it was killing *American* boys. They shed few tears for the two million Vietnamese, including half a million children, killed in their own country by the US war machine.

During an ascendancy that now spans at least two hundred years, the West has done little to forge a single humanity that embraces all the peoples of the world. For the most part, Western thinkers have pursued their humanist ideals within the paradigms of race and tribe. With few exceptions, the Enlightenment thinkers refused to share

2 Pervez Hoodbhoy "Muslims and the West after September 11," *Dawn*, December 10 and 11, 2001.

their humanity with Africans, Amerindians, Aborigines or Asians. Racism was germane to the thinking of the leading Western humanists, not excluding the great Montesquieu, Hume, Kant and Jefferson.[3] Even as they glorified 'man,' they saw little that was wrong in colonialism, slavery or the massacres of 'uncivilized tribes,' 'barbarians' and 'savages.' Europe's dream of reason did not produce sweetness and light for Amerindians, Africans, Asians or the 'outsiders' in Europe itself.

A Matter of Timing

I will turn directly to Hoodbhoy's Orientalist thesis on the decline of Islamicate societies: his rejection of Islam hinges on this theory.

First, he is quite wrong about the timing of this decline. He claims that Islam lost its creative élan in the thirteenth century, a result of the twin blows dealt by the 'ulama – the jurisprudents and theologians of Islam – and the Mongols. This suggests that Hoodbhoy has been raised on a rather pure diet of Orientalism and its falsification of Islamicate history.

Hoodbhoy employs graphic imagery in presenting his ideas. Islam was "choked" in the twelfth century by the "vice-like grip of orthodoxy" created by the anti-rationalism of Ghazali, whom he describes, incorrectly, as a "cleric." He also refers to the "trauma" of the thirteenth century. Presumably, he is referring to the Mongol destruction of Baghdad in 1258.

Bernard Lewis, the dean of the post-war generation of Zionist Orientalists – and, probably, an important source of Hoodbhoy's inspiration – places the Islamicate decline even earlier. Although "signs of decadence are visible even earlier," he declares that by the

---

[3] Emmanuel Eze, *Race and Enlightenment: A Reader* (Blackwell: 2000).

eleventh century "the world of Islam was in a state of *manifest* decay (emphasis added)."[4] He accomplishes this *tour de force* – establishing the early decline of the Islamicate world – by equating Islamicate civilization with Arab power.

It is odd that after its "manifest decay," Islamicate power, barring the reversal in Spain, continued to expand for several more centuries. In the Levant, the Muslims contained the repeated onslaughts of the Crusaders over two centuries, finally expelling them in 1291. The Ottomans expanded into the Balkans, taking Constantinople in 1453, and twice laid siege to Vienna, the second time in 1683. In the West, the Berbers extended Islamicate power into Sub-Saharan Africa. Perhaps most importantly, once the Turks and Mongols entered Islam, Islamicate power extended deep into Central Asia, up the Volga River, beyond the Tarim Basin, and past the Hindu Kush into the plains of North India. In addition, Arab and Persian traders were seeding Islamicate communities in East Africa, southern India, and the islands of the Indonesian archipelago.

Marshall Hodgson has challenged the Orientalist canard about an early decline of Islamicate civilization in *The Venture of Islam* (1974), a deep, sweeping and multi-faceted account of the history and civilization of Islamicate societies. He has written that, "in its own setting, the age of the sixteenth and seventeenth centuries was one of the greatest in Islamdom's history. The artistic, philosophic, and social power and creativeness of the age can be symbolized in the spaciousness, purity – and overwhelming magnificence of the Tâj Mahall at Agra. In some sense there was a great florescence."[5] The Isphahan School of philosophy, founded by Mulla Sadra (d.

---

4 Bernard Lewis, "The Arabs in Eclipse," in: Carlo M. Cippola, ed., *The Economic Decline of Empires* (London: Methuen, 1970): 102.

5 Marshall G. S. Hodgson, *The Venture of Islam*, Volume 3 (Chicago: University of Chicago Press, 1974): 14.

1640), is now recognized by Western authorities as a major philosophical movement.[6]

Scientific activity in the Islamicate world did not face sudden death either. George Saliba, a leading historian of Islamicate science, extends the Islamicate golden age to the fifteenth century.[7] Soon after their conquest of much of the central Islamicate lands, the Mongols turned their energies to rebuilding the societies they had destroyed. In fact, several of them took up earnestly the patronage of the arts and sciences, and major observatories were being set up as late as the fifteenth century. The astronomical tables computed at these observatories, together with the work of Ibn-Shatir (d. 1375), a time-keeper in the central mosque of Damascus, were passed on to Europe, and are believed to have contributed to the Copernican Revolution. Western debt to Islamicate sciences – in the fields of mathematics, optics, astronomy and medicine – may turn out to be deeper yet, once historians take up the research into these connections more seriously.

If there was a falling off in the scientific output of Islamicate societies after the eleventh century, this was compensated by growing activity in a variety of other human endeavors, including historiography, poetry, architecture, painting and – in Iran – philosophy. Given this, it is a bit silly to scapegoat Ghazali for "choking" Islam with his "vice-like grip" of orthodoxy. In fact, Ghazali was a major philosopher in his own right whose philosophical skepticism anticipated Descartes and Kant; but unlike them, he turned to spiritual empiricism to transcend his doubts. Ghazali attacked the heterodox Isma'ilis and the heretical tendencies among Muslims who delved in Greek metaphysics. He was not opposed to logic, mathematics or the sciences.

---

6 Henry Corbin, *History of Islamic Philosophy* (London: Kegan Paul, 1993).

7 George Saliba, *A History of Arabic Astronomy* (New York University Press: 1994): 7.

Rise of Western Europe

If it was not in the eleventh or twelfth centuries, when did the decline of Islamicate societies become manifest? We must look for the beginnings of this process, as well as its source, not so much in Islamicate societies as in Western Europe. It was Western Europe that gathered speed and moved ahead of *all* other societies, starting in the fifteenth century. In turn, the ascendancy of the West produced decline and decay in nearly all non-Western societies, not only those in the Islamicate world.

Western Europe's ascendancy began with its lead in two critical areas, gunnery and shipping, starting in the fifteenth century. The West Europeans did not invent gunpowder and cannons; both are Chinese inventions that were diffused to Europe and the Middle East by the invading Mongols in the thirteenth century. However, the constantly warring Europeans soon took the lead – because of their more decentralized polity – in improving gunpowder weaponry; this included lighter cannons and handguns. At the same time, the Western Europeans were building sturdier ships to negotiate the stormy Baltic Sea and the Atlantic Ocean. In the fifteenth century, when the Western Europeans mounted their light cannons on their sturdy ships, this combination proved deadly against the galleys of the Mediterranean and the flimsier ships of the generally calm Indian Ocean. Luck also favored Europe. In 1433, the Chinese not only withdrew their maritime presence from the Indian Ocean, they scrapped their fleet of superior ships. This was a fateful measure. If the Chinese had continued their maritime explorations, they would have challenged the European entry into the Indian Ocean. It is even likely that they would be 'discovering' Europe, instead of the other way around.

This superiority in gunnery and shipping launched Atlantic Europe, through deepening cycles of cumulative causation, on the path of global ascendancy. Its first dividend was the 'discovery' of the Americas, perhaps the greatest resource windfall ever received by any society. This was quickly followed by the European passage into the Indian Ocean, which led to a growing monopoly over the trade of the Indian Ocean, easily the world's richest trading area. In addition, America's gold and silver gave an economically backward Europe the means for entering into the trade of the Indian Ocean. In the long run, Europe's command of the high seas produced vast new sources of wealth through plunder, trade, shipping, banking and overseas investments; and, in turn, the growth of shipping and commerce stimulated manufactures. When some of this new wealth was used to support universities and academies, it produced a growing interest in philosophy, mathematics and the sciences. Directly and indirectly, these advances contributed to Europe's military technology, which, in turn, expanded their overseas empires and brought still greater profits. By the beginning of the nineteenth century – in India before that – these developments had come to a head. Europe was ready to start its project of dismantling Islamicate empires and states in the Mediterranean and the Indian Ocean.

Why did the Islamicate – or other Asian and African – polities fail to resist this growing European thrust? The Eurocentric narratives insist that Europe's ascendancy since the sixteenth century is not new. It was only the latest expression, now played out on the global stage, of the superiority that Europe has always enjoyed over other civilizations. Europe's superiority shows itself in stronger rationality, individualism, vigor, enterprise, love of freedom and curiosity. These perennial tendencies are gifts of divine Providence, a superior biological endowment, a diverse and more generous topography, or a more invigorating climate. In blaming Ghazali – read Islam – for the decline of Islamicate societies, Hoodbhoy is buying into the Weberian version of this Eurocentric narrative, which identifies Western ascendancy with the greater rationality promoted by Protestantism.

A historical narrative – one that is rooted in cumulative processes, contingencies, conjunctures, contradictions, accidents and unintended consequences – tells a different story. The colonization of the Americas, the growing control over the trade of the Indian Ocean, the mercantilist rivalries and incessant wars among European states – produced by the anarchy of their decentralized political system – accelerated the dynamic of historical change in Europe, allowing it to outpace the more centralized, mostly land-based empires of the Middle East, India and China. In the long run, the Netherlands, Britain, France and the United States slowly built upon their successes in commerce, shipping, the arts of warfare, state-formation and manufactures to develop into centers of capitalist production, which drew their economic strength from an alliance between capital and the state.

Globally, the growth of these centers of capitalist production – the Core of the world economy – produced, simultaneously, their opposite and complement, an underdeveloped Periphery, dominated by capital from the Core and restructured to supply raw materials – in some cases, labor – to the Core countries. In most cases, the loss of sovereignty preceded or accompanied a country's incorporation into the Periphery. With the solitary exception of Japan, the leading Core countries converted the non-White countries into outright colonies or forced them to sign open-door treaties, which gave preferential treatment to Core capital. However, most countries of European ethnicity in the Periphery – for reasons of geopolitics and heritage – retained much of their sovereignty. These countries exercised various degrees of sovereign control over their economic policies to promote indigenous capital and technology. In the long haul, some of them pulled out of the Periphery to join the Core.[8]

Quite a few historians and sociologists attribute the ascendancy of Western Europe to its greater rationality, a legacy thought to derive from its cultivation of Greek philosophy. This is spurious history and false sociology – two unavoidable ingredients of all Eurocentric thought. The truth is quite the opposite of this. The verdict of Ernest Gellner, a philosopher and social anthropologist, deserves to be quoted in full: "By various obvious criteria – universalism, scripturalism, spiritual egalitarianism, the extension of full participation in the sacred community not to one, or some, but to *all*, and the rational systematization of social life – Islam is, of the three great Western monotheisms, the closest to modernity."[9] The French sociologist, Maxine Rodinson, arrived at a similar conclusion when he examined the precepts of Islam in relation to the demands of a capitalist system.[10]

In addition, the standard claims about the rationality of modern Europe – even during the Enlightenment – are exaggerated. Several of the leading scientists of the seventeenth century – including Tycho Brahe, Galileo Galilei, Johannes Kepler and Pierre Gassendi – admired for their contributions to the development of modern physics and astronomy, held astrology in high esteem. Even Isaac Newton, perhaps the greatest scientist of modern times, devoted nearly two decades of his life to investigations in alchemy. A mere twelve percent of the books in Newton's personal library were on physics, astronomy and mathematics. On the contrary, not only were the

[8] M. Shahid Alam, *Poverty from the Wealth of Nations* (Houndmills, UK: Palgrave Macmillan, 2000).

[9] Ernest Gellner, *Muslim Society* (Cambridge, UK: Cambridge University Press: 1981): 7.

[10] Maxine Rodinson, *Islam and Capitalism* (Austin, TX: University of Texas Press: 1978).

leading philosopher-scientists of Islamicate societies opposed to astrology, so was Islamic orthodoxy.

Failing to Recoup the Losses

This brings us to the failure of Islamicate societies – a problem not shared by India or China – to mount an adequate recovery from the losses of the colonial epoch.

The European empires established in the nineteenth century did not last very long – as empires go. Their racist, exploitative, and sometimes genocidal policies fuelled vigorous anti-imperialist movements across much of Asia, Africa and the Caribbean. In time, the colonial powers got into two major brawls – better known as the two World Wars – accelerating their own demise. The First World War created an opening for the emergence of the world's first anti-capitalist regime in Russia; the Second World War did the same in China. In addition, the Second World War crystallized a new power structure, dominated by the United States and the Soviet Union, each opposed for different reasons to the old colonial empires. As the leading capitalist economy, the United States was jealous of the privileged access the colonial powers had to their colonies. The Soviet Union contested the capitalist powers by supporting radical and nationalist movements in the colonies. In other words, the conditions were ripe for the dismantling of colonial empires at the end of the Second World War.

The end of colonial era, however, did not herald a bright future for all subject populations. In particular, the Islamicate world that emerged from the colonial era was weak and fragmented. It lacked a core state; the colonial powers had splintered the Arabs into some thirty states, some of them little more than collections of oil wells; Britain and the United States had placed the oil-rich states under despotic monarchies; and the Zionists had established a Jewish state in nearly all of Palestine. In contrast, India and China were decidedly better off. The Indians entered the new era with great hopes. Only for the third time in their long history, the Hindus were in charge of a united India, the second largest country in the world that appeared poised to rise to the ranks of a great power. India was in capable hands too; its leaders were committed to democracy and keenly aware of the unique moment in their history. In addition, after nearly two centuries of colonial rule, the Indian economy was mostly in the hands of indigenous capital. China too had emerged single and whole – but for the loss of Taiwan, Hong Kong and Macao – having fought off a succession of imperialist powers and indigenous centrifugal forces. In 1948, after nearly a century of civil wars and the depredations of Europeans, Americans and Japanese, the long-suffering Chinese reconstituted their ancient Confucian state under new forms. The imperial house and the mandarins gave way to a communist party forged through decades of struggle against Chinese warlords and foreign imperialists.

The Islamicate world commanded at least three major empires in 1600: the Ottoman, Safavid and Mughal. At the time, and for several more decades, the Ottomans alone could stand up to the forces assembled by any combination of the leading European states. Yet none of the post-colonial Islamicate states could aspire to the power that belonged to these empires. Why had Islamicate societies failed to reconstitute their former power in the post-colonial period? It is important to answer this question, since this *political* failure lies at the root of the present troubles in the Islamicate world. The Orientalists who claim that the turbulence in the Islamicate world is born from a failure of modernity are inverting the order of causation.

As recently as 1750, Islamicate power stretched from Mauritania and the Balkans in the West to Indonesia and Mindanao in East Asia.

However, this power lacked an enduring demographic base. In the Balkans and India, the Ottomans and the Mughals ruled over non-Muslim majorities. Once nationalist consciousness gained ground as the principal basis of statehood, the Ottoman Empire lost its legitimacy, challenged first by its Christian population in Europe and later by Arab fellow Muslims who resented domination by the Ottoman Turks. In India, Hindu resentment against their Muslim rulers accelerated the dissolution of the Mughal Empire, and, later, the defeat of Muslim successor states in the face of British competition. Importantly, once these Islamicate Empires disintegrated, it would be nearly impossible to reconstitute them in the absence of a Muslim majority.

The Islamicate societies suffered from a second demographic handicap in their struggle against European imperialism. Once the Middle East had lost the momentum of an early start with the agricultural revolution, the population advantage shifted to China, India and Europe. Indeed, after the first century of the Common Era, the region even failed to maintain its absolute population. As a result, the population of the region in 1800 was considerably smaller than it was in ancient times or the early Islamicate period. More ominously, the total population of North Africa, Egypt, the Fertile Crescent and Arabia in 1800 was only modestly ahead of the population of France. In other words, these central Islamicate regions lacked both demographic weight and geographic depth – since this population was strung out along the Mediterranean coast and two river valleys – in its vital contest with expansionist European powers. Given this demographic disproportion, some Europeans dreamed of eradicating the Islamic character of North Africa and the Levant with a little help from colonial settlers.

The Islamicate states bordering the Mediterranean faced another handicap: they were only a few days' sail from Europe. This made them tempting targets for European capital and cupidity, mixed with some of the old Christian zeal for eradicating Islam. France, Britain, the Zionists and Italy took up this project successively. The French proceeded to colonize Algeria, Tunisia and Morocco, and quickly introduced white settlers with the aim of annexing these regions to France. The European powers dismantled the Egyptian effort to industrialize – initiated by Muhammad Ali Pasha in 1810 – after they intervened to block his march on Istanbul in 1839. When the Egyptians mobilized again in the 1870s to assert their independence, the British occupied Egypt in 1882. Taking advantage of the First World War, Britain and France occupied the Arab territories of the Ottoman Empire and carved them into several small states, with one slice going to the Zionists, as promised in the Balfour Declaration of 1917. Britain, France and Israel mounted another invasion of Egypt in 1956, roiled when Gamal Nasser nationalized the Suez Canal. Luckily, the United States was not too pleased over this European adventure, and the invasion was called off in a hurry.

This capsule history of the Middle East offers some sobering reflections for the Eurocentrists and their Muslim acolytes who attribute the backwardness of Islamicate societies to their religion and culture: to Islam's antipathy to science, rationality and modernity. Imagine just one counterfactual. Imagine if the Egyptian bid to industrialize had *not* been dismantled by the European powers. It is then likely that an industrialized Egypt would have become a catalyst for industrial transformation in other Middle Eastern countries. This thought experiment explains why the Europeans united to abort Muhammad Ali Pasha's industrial drive. An industrialized Middle East would have renewed the old threat of Islam to Europe.

On the other hand, the European powers showed little interest in blocking Japan's industrial drive initiated some sixty years after Egypt's. Japan succeeded because it was an archipelago tethered off the eastern edge of Asia, half a world away from Western Europe and separated from the United States by the vast Pacific Ocean. Of equal importance, Japan's mix of Shinto and Confucian culture did not set off alarms in the European psyche. Could Japan have pulled off its industrial coup if it had been a Muslim island anchored in the Eastern Mediterranean or even the Arabian Sea?

The impotence of Arabs in the post-colonial period goes back to three additional factors: Zionism, the old Christian vendetta against Islam, and oil. The Zionists founded their project on a confluence of Jewish and Western interests in the Middle East. The Zionists proposed to rid Europe of Jews if Europe would help them to establish a Jewish state in Palestine. In succession, Zionist ambitions combined with European Islamophobia to produce the Balfour Declaration of 1917, the dismantling of the Ottoman Empire, the vivisection of the former Ottoman territories in the Fertile Crescent, the creation of a Maronite-dominated mini-state in Lebanon, the British mandate over Palestine, and the creation of a Jewish colonial-settler state in Arab Palestine. Arab aspirations in the Fertile Crescent had been dealt a body blow from which it would be hard to recover. Had the Arabs of this region been free to realize their nationalist aspirations, most likely they would have created a single Arab state that might well have included – because of its religious significance – the Arabian Peninsula as well, or at least the Hejaz and the oil-rich Gulf coast.

In the meanwhile, the United States and Britain were negotiating arrangements in the Persian Gulf to ensure Western control over the richest oil reserves in the world. They decided to place the region under archaic, absolutist monarchies whose survival, against the rising tide of nationalism, would depend on the United States. As part of this plan, when a democratic movement overthrew the Iranian monarchy in 1953, the United States and Britain orchestrated a coup to re-instate the monarchy. In 1967, Israel inflicted a humiliating defeat on Egypt and Syria – leading to the occupation of Sinai, the

Golan Heights, the West Bank and Gaza – virtually removing the Arab nationalist challenge to Western control over Middle Eastern oil. The Middle East straightjacket was now securely in place.

While appreciating the global forces arrayed against them, it is disconcerting to watch the ease with which the Arabs, the peoples no less than their leaders, have slipped into the straitjacket prepared for them by the Western imperialists. In the final analysis, the historical verdict on the Arab national awakening is clear: it failed. While the leaders of the Arab nationalist movements created a discourse of Arab nationalism – a concept of nationhood founded on language and history – they failed to create a deep consciousness of Arab unity, one that would seek its goal in Arab political unity, in a single Arab statehood. Once the Arab nationalists had gained power over Egypt, Syria and Iraq towards the end of the 1950s, their failure to realize a political unity – apart from a short-lived union between Egypt and Syria – is testimony to the tenuous character of the Arab nationalist project. Not even the successive defeats inflicted by Israel on various combinations of Arab states – in 1948, 1956 and 1967 – could create the impetus for unity, the desire to restore Arab honor, or mobilize to face the massive threat that Israel posed to Arab security. Arab nationalism was mostly talk – rhetoric without substance.

The Iranian revolution of 1979 failed to loosen the Western stranglehold on the Middle East. On the contrary, by raising the specter of Islamist power in the region, this paved the way for an 'Arab' war against Iran – with funding from the Gulf Arabs, manpower from Egypt, and the blessings of Western powers – to contain the spread of the Islamist revolution to the Arab countries. In time, after the collapse of the Soviet Union, the corrupt Arab regimes formed a grand alliance – under the aegis of the United States and Israel – to control and repress their Islamist movements. In 1993, the

Palestine Liberation Organization recognized Israel and agreed to police the Palestinian Islamists in return for municipal control over parts of the West Bank and Gaza. Syria and Libya chose to repress their Islamists without joining this alliance; as a result, the United States placed them in the limbo of 'rogue states.' When foolhardy Iraq dared to challenge this alliance in 1990, without the nerve to carry it to completion, it was bombed back to the Stone Age and crippled with comprehensive economic sanctions.

A new imperialism had descended on the Islamicate world in the 1990s. Its rules were clear. The United States would support despots in the Muslim states so long as they came to terms with Israel and kept a tight lid on political Islam. If any country dared to depart from the terms of this contract, it faced economic sanctions – and, if these did not work, war. When Iraq challenged this contract in 1990, it faced both endless war and crippling sanctions that have devastated its economy and caused more than a million deaths. Similarly, Algeria illustrates the fate awaiting a Muslim country if the Islamists seek to capture power – even through the democratic process.

This new imperialist contract explains why the 'democratization' of the 1990s bypassed much of the Islamicate world. Professor Hoodbhoy thinks otherwise. Instead of offering a historical analysis, rooted in the dynamics of global capitalism and the legacy of past conflicts between Europe and the Islamicate world, he joins the Orientalists in blaming the difficulties of the Islamicate world on Islam, the religion and civilization. His method is familiar – damnation by accusation, damnation by defining the essence of Islamicate societies. If Islam is obscurantist, anti-rationalist, fanatical, and misogynist, *then* we can explain the aversion of the Islamicate world towards modernity and democracy. The Orientalist has spoken: the case is closed.

Those who maintain that Islam is anti-democratic might gain from a short lesson in the modern history of constitutional movements in Islamicate countries. Muhammad Ali of Egypt appointed his first advisory council in 1824, consisting mostly of elected members. In 1881, the Egyptian nationalists succeeded in convening an elected parliament, but the British disbanded this when they occupied Egypt a year later. Tunisia had promulgated a constitution in 1860, setting up a Supreme Council purporting to limit the powers of the monarchy. However, the French suppressed this Council in 1864 when they discovered that it interfered with their ambitions in Tunisia. Turkey elected its first parliament in 1877 though it was dissolved a year later by the Caliph; a second parliament was convened in 1908. Iran's progress was more dramatic. It started with protests against the grant of a British tobacco monopoly in the 1890s, but this escalated into demands for a constitutional monarchy. In 1906, Iran's first elected parliament adopted a constitution limiting the powers of the monarchy and assumed the power to confirm the cabinet. However, this led to a struggle between the Qajar rulers and the constitutionalists. In 1911, with support from their Russian and British patrons, the Qajar monarch defeated the Constitutionalists and disbanded the parliament. The Constitutional movement persisted for two more decades, until the new Pahlavi dynasty, which rose to power with help from the British, suppressed it in 1931.

Compare these developments with the history of constitutional movements elsewhere, not excluding Europe, during the nineteenth century – and the world of Islam does not suffer from the comparison. Incredible as this appears to minds blinded by Eurocentric prejudice, Tunisia, Egypt and Iran were taking the lead in making the transition to constitutional monarchies. In recent decades too, democracy in the region has not been stifled by some essential incompatibility between democracy and Arab or Islamic traditions. Both directly and indirectly, oil, Israel and the old Western antipathy to Islam have been important factors derailing the normal evolution of these societies. Oil led to British and, later, US support for monarchies and dictatorships that suppressed the nationalist and democratic aspirations of their people. The insertion of Israel – an expansionist, colonial-settler state – into the region produced wars and tensions, which supported the creation of security states at the cost of civil society. More recently, the growth of an Islamist opposition has deepened Western support for repressive regimes in the region.

A US-Imposed Straightjacket

The US-imposed straightjacket has deepened the contradictions of global capitalism in the Islamicate world: a development that is pregnant with consequences that threaten to spin out of control.

During the Cold War, the dominant factions in many Third World countries competed with each other to win the US contract for repressing their radical and populist movements. As long as they did their job, these repressive regimes enjoyed a degree of autonomy in managing their economies. Taking advantage of this autonomy, many Third World countries implemented interventionist policies to develop indigenous capital and technology. A few of them in East Asia, those most favored by the United States, became showcases of capitalist success. When the Soviet Union collapsed in 1990, the United States terminated this Cold War contract. It was replaced by the Washington Consensus, which called upon the countries in the Periphery to open up their economies to Core capital. The World Trade Organization was created to formalize the new arrangements, which were a great deal more comprehensive than the Open Door treaties imposed on nominally independent countries in the nineteenth century. The elites in the Periphery quickly got the message.

Soon they were competing to open up their economies for takeover by multinational corporations.

The United States offered two versions of this new colonial contract. Countries in the non-Islamicate Periphery are generally encouraged to compete for the contract through the ballot box. In countries that have strong Islamist movements, this option is not available; their dictators and monarchs are employed to keep the lid on Islamist movements. The excuse for this two-track policy is flimsy. Western commentators argue that the Islamist parties will only use the ballot to abolish democracy once they gain an electoral majority. The real reason is Western nervousness over the Islamist's twin goals: introducing an Islamic social order and reversing the fragmentation and marginalization of Islamicate societies. Washington has decided that it will oppose and suppress the Islamists at all costs.

The US-Israeli siege of the Islamicate world is unlikely to deliver peace to the region. On the contrary, it has engendered contradictions that will only deepen over time. After the Israeli rout of the Arab armies in 1967, secular Arab nationalism stood discredited: not only had it failed to unite the Arabs to reclaim Palestine, it had lost more Arab lands to Israel. Having depleted their political capital and, therefore, the support of their people, the Arab regimes were now ready for deals with Washington and Tel Aviv. In 1973, with appropriate cash rewards from the US, Egypt made a separate peace with Israel. In abdicating its leadership of the Arab world, Egypt wrote the obituary of Arab nationalism. Only the Islamists could now assume the historic task of liberating and uniting the Arab world.

Although humiliated, the Arab regimes remained firmly ensconced in power. In large part, this was a gift of the new colonial contract. The United States encouraged the Arab regimes – with intelligence, technology and loans when needed – to compensate for their loss of legitimacy by tightening their repressive regimes. The turn around from a strident Arab nationalism to capitulation was quick, moving through abdication at Camp David, concessions at Oslo, normalization of ties with Israel, and the embrace of the Washington Consensus. On the domestic front, these regimes intensified the repression of their Islamist opposition. They banned the Islamist parties, removed the Islamists from leading positions in professional associations and trade unions, and eventually the leading Islamists were jailed, executed or hounded out of the country.

This repression of Islamists has produced two results. Nearly everywhere, the Arab regimes blocked Islamists who wished to work through the institutions of civil society, including political parties, professional associations, the media, courts and charities. This shifted the focus to radical Islamists, those who were willing to engage in violent actions – guerilla war, assassinations and terror – to gain their ends. However, even the radicals had little leeway under the repressive Arab regimes. Those who evaded capture or execution went underground or escaped to Afghanistan, Pakistan or the Western countries. At some point, some radical Islamists decided to change their strategy. They would target their problems at their source – and inflict damage on the United States. They decided to sting the United States into lifting its siege of Islamicate countries. Alternatively, they hoped to provoke wars – like the one in Afghanistan – on the chance that this would stir radicalism and revolutions against neocolonial surrogates in the Islamicate world.

There are powerful economic forces that affect this dynamic. I will mention one: the brain drain that has accelerated with the growing mobility of skilled workers. The range of deleterious economic and social effects produced by brain drain has received little attention from social scientists. Perhaps, the most talented members of the work force now migrate to developed countries. This drains the developing countries of their best doctors, engineers and scientists: an all too familiar phenomenon. In addition, the brain drain depletes a country of its leaders, activists, scholars, poets, and its conscience. Over the past two decades, this has greatly weakened the progressive forces in nearly all the countries of the Periphery.

Almost as damaging, the brain drain leaves a second layer of alienation in its wake. Those who succeed in leaving are only a fraction of those who *want* to leave and who, therefore, order their lives around the chance of leaving. As a result, the college graduates who stay at home – because they cannot yet leave – remain disconnected from their own societies. This has had a deadening effect on mechanisms for social change, deepening the vicious circle of poverty, social apathy and corruption.

All of this has slowly produced a coarsening of the Islamic discourse in some Islamicate countries. The brain drain has contributed to a growing lumpenization of the Islamist opposition. As more people from the middle classes exercise the exit option, the intellectual and political leadership of the Islamist movements has passed into the hands of persons who have little chance of taking the exit option. Increasingly, the Islamist leaders come from marginalized classes – including shopkeepers, clerks and self-employed workers – who are excluded from the exit option by their education in the vernaculars or religious schools. These Islamists are busy creating a militant Jihadi culture in Pakistan, Algeria, Indonesia and Afghanistan.

Giving Up 'False Notions'?

Pervez Hoodbhoy counsels Muslims to give up the 'false notions' of Islam.[11] On the contrary, Muslims alienated from their roots need to

---

[11] The second part of Hoodbhoy's essay appeared under the title: "Time To Give Up False Notions."

renounce false Orientalist narratives – of an Islam that has been misrepresented as irrational, misogynist, fatalist and fanatical.

Rational thinking did not begin with the Enlightenment. In fact, several Enlightenment thinkers turned to Islam to advance their own struggle against medieval obscurantism, the intolerance of an organized clergy, and the anti-rationalism of their own mystery religion. According to Bernard Lewis, "The image of Mohammed as a wise, tolerant, unmystical and undogmatic ruler became widespread in the period of the Enlightenment."[12] It is time for alienated Muslim intellectuals to tear the Orientalist veil that obscures their vision of Islam, re-enter the historical currents they have abandoned, create a deeper understanding of the dynamics of derailed Islamicate societies, and lead them into an *Islamic* vision of a world where all communities, ethnic and religious, race against each other "in doing good works."[13] After more than eighty years of Kemalism, a military clique still calls the shots in secular Turkey, wages war against a fifth of its own population, trembles at the sight of women in scarves, and grovels to gain entry into the margins of European society. Do we want to litter the Islamicate landscape with yet more half-baked Turkeys?

The West too must overcome its false notions of the Islamicate world as the irreconcilable 'Other', the fundamental peril that must forever be opposed, fought against, bottled and besieged. If Islamicate societies appear to be a greater threat to the West than India or China, that is because the actions of Western powers, now and in the past, as well as the forces of history, geography and demography,

---

[12] *Islam and the West* (Oxford University Press: 1993): 90.

[13] This refers to the following verse from the Qur'ān: "For each We have appointed a divine law and a traced-out way. Had Allah willed He could have made you one community. But that He may try you by that which He hath given you (He hath made you as ye are). So vie one with another in good works. Unto Allah will ye return, and He will then inform you of that wherein ye differ." (5:48)."

have fragmented Islamicate societies and, so far, prevented them from reconstituting their center, their wholeness and history. Nearly a fourth of the world's peoples seek their identity and dignity, their place in this world and the next, within a stream of history that flows from the Qur'ān. They want to live by ethical ideals that have produced the austere nobility of the Prophet's companions, an egalitarianism that elevated slaves to kingship, the juristic insights of Al Shafi'i and Abu Hanifa, the mystical flights of Al-Arabi and Rumi, the rationalism of Ibn Rushd and Ibn Tufail, the mathematics of Al-Khawarizmi and Khayyam, the scientific achievements of Ibn Sina and Al-Haytham, the sociological insights of Ibn Khaldun and Al-Biruni, the majesty of Al-Hambra and the Taj, the observatories of Samarqand and Maragha, the tolerance of Salahuddin and Akbar, and the poetry of Rumi, Hafiz, Ghalib and Iqbal. Once they regain their autonomy, dignity and integrity, the Islamicate societies can again produce another cultural efflorescence that draws upon the light, freshness and sweetness of the Qur'ān. The Qur'ānic impulse towards truth, justice, sincerity and beauty will find expression again, not in combat, but in a new Arabesque of creative minds and soulful hearts, intertwined with reason and mercy.

CHAPTER TWO

How Different are Islamicate Societies?

"O mankind! Be careful of your duty to your Lord Who created you from a single soul and from it created its mate and from them twain hath spread abroad a multitude of men and women."

Qur'ān: 4:1

February 4, 2002

There are two opposite visions that animate American scholarship on Islam and Islamicate societies. In the days, months and years ahead, a great deal will hinge on which of these visions informs American foreign policy.

One vision represents Islam – the religion and society – as an enemy that must be destroyed, or it will destroy the West. This is the camp of warriors, led, among others, by Bernard Lewis, Daniel Pipes, Charles Krauthammer and Martin Kramer. Their thinking is reductionist and ahistorical; they believe that Islam is fundamentally at odds with the core values of the West. These warriors urge the United States to confront this menace now and contain it militarily before it threatens Western dominance.

The second vision proposes that Islamicate societies are diverse, containing tendencies – religious, cultural and political – that pull in different directions. It argues that political Islam does not reject modernity; instead, it seeks to indigenize modernity, to give it a local habitation and a name. This is the diplomatic camp, led, among others, by John Esposito, Richard Bulliet and Bruce Lawrence. They believe in engaging Islamist movements, giving them a chance to run Islamicate societies since this will either discredit them or bring them into the political mainstream.

It is worth noting that, in the world of scholarship, the warriors are a minority. However, together with their neoconservative allies, they enjoy considerably greater political and media clout than the diplomatic camp. This clout had been increasing since the end of the Cold War. And now, after September 11, President Bush appears to be embracing their objective of waging pre-emptive wars against major Islamicate countries. At the present juncture, laden with tensions, it would be all too easy to start these wars; but, once started, they may be harder to stop.

I will review some of the charges leveled by the camp of warriors against Islamicate societies. Are Islamicate societies lagging in economic development; do they face a clear democracy deficit; and do they have "bloody borders," a phrase coined by Samuel Huntington? Contrary to popular perceptions, the evidence fails to support these charges.

Economic Development

The Islamicate world does face any number of serious problems: it would be foolish to deny this. What we need to determine is whether Islamicate countries have done worse, or much worse, than others with a comparable history in pursuing economic growth, promoting equality between the sexes, developing free institutions, and keeping the peace with its neighbors?

First, consider the question of economic development. Judging from their living standards in 1999, measured as per capita income in international dollars – taken from the *World Development Report, 2000* – it does not appear that Muslims have done too badly.[1] In several paired comparisons, Iran holds its own against Venezuela, Malaysia is well ahead of Thailand, Egypt is modestly ahead of Ukraine, Turkey only slightly behind Russia, Pakistan a little behind – and Indonesia somewhat ahead – of India, Bangladesh is somewhat behind Vietnam, Tunisia is well ahead of Georgia and Armenia, and Jordan is significantly ahead of Nicaragua. It is important to note that some of the comparisons concede the historical advantage to the non-Islamicate countries that gained their independence earlier.

The results do not change if we base the comparisons on a broader human development index. In a ranking that includes 162 countries in 1999 – taken from the *Human Development Report, 2000* – 22 Islamicate countries occupy ranks between 32 and 100.[2] Pakistan, Bangladesh and Sudan rank lower down the scale, but they are still ahead of several non-Islamicate countries in Africa. Notably, the Arab oil-rich countries are the leaders of the Islamicate pack. Incredibly, Saudi Arabia, the bastion of conservative Islam, spends 7.5 percent of its national income on public education; this places it in the same class as Norway and Finland.

The evidence does confirm the charge of a gender bias in Islamicate countries. Nearly half of them show gender bias in their development indices. We observe that 17 of the 36 Islamicate countries suffer a loss of rank as we move from a general index of human development to one that makes corrections for inequalities between sexes; both indices are available in the latest *Human Development Report*. These losses are highest for Saudi Arabia, Yemen, Oman,

---

[1] World Bank, *World Development Report, 2000* (New York: Oxford University Press, 2000).

[2] UNDP, *Human Development Report, 2000* (New York: Oxford University Press, 2000).

Sudan and Lebanon. Only Turkey improves its rank significantly, by four places.

The cultural determinism of the warriors extends to demographics. Observing the rapid growth of Islamicate population, they attribute this to a cultural resistance to birth control. Once again, an examination of the evidence quickly dispels this charge. Between 1970-75 and 1995-2000, nearly every Islamicate country experienced a decline in the total fertility rate: this is the number of childbirths per woman over her lifetime. In several, the decline was quite impressive. The fertility rates for 1995-2000 were 1.9 in Azerbaijan, 2.3 in Tunisia, 2.6 in Indonesia, 3.2 in Iran, 3.3 in Malaysia and Algeria, and 3.4 in Morocco and Egypt: compared to 3.3 and 3.6 for India and Philippines respectively. The Islamicate countries reached these low rates of fertility over shorter periods than Europe or Latin America.

Bloody Borders

We now turn to the matter about the "bloody borders" of Islamicate societies. In his book, *The Clash of Civilizations*, Samuel Huntington claims that "Muslim bellicosity and violence are late-twentieth century facts which neither Muslims nor non-Muslims can deny."[3] In support of this thesis, he offers a list of inter-civilizational conflicts affecting Islamicate borders in the 1990s. He also provides some quantitative evidence purporting to show that Muslims had a disproportionate share in inter-civilizational conflicts during 1993-94.

A more careful examination of the data tells a different story. Jonathan Fox has shown that Islam was involved in 23.2 percent of all inter-civilizational conflicts between 1945 and 1989, and 24.7

---

[3] Samuel P. Huntington, *The Clash of Civilizations and the Remaking of World Order* (New York: Simon and Schuster, 1996): 258.

percent of these conflicts during 1990 to 1998.[4] This is not too far above Islam's share in world population; nor do we observe any dramatic rise in this share since the end of the Cold War. It would appear that Huntington's claims of "Muslim bellicosity" do not qualify as facts.

In any case, we have to be careful when we talk about "bloody borders." A hard look at the geography of civilizations soon reveals that civilizational borders vary strikingly, and that the Islamicate share of such borders is disproportionately large. On the one hand, the geographic sweep of the Islamicate societies across the Afro-Eurasian landmass brings it into contact – both close and extensive – with the African, Western, Orthodox, Hindu and Buddhist civilizations. We must contend not only with borders between Islamicate and non-Islamicate countries. In addition, we must take account of the internal borders, between Muslim and non-Muslim populations within non-Islamicate countries. It is my impression that if we added up all of these borders, the Islamicate share of borders might well exceed the combined share of all other civilizations. These facts might help to place observations about Islam's "bloody borders" in a less prejudicial perspective.

The Democracy Deficit

Finally, there is the charge of a democracy deficit in the Islamicate world. Several warriors, including Samuel Huntington and Elie Kedourie, have theorized that this is because of an incompatibility between Islamic values and democratic institutions.[5]

The warriors find evidence of a democracy deficit in Islamicate

---

[4] Jonathan Fox, "Two Civilizations and Ethnic Conflict: Islam and the West," *Journal of Peace Research* 38, 4 (2000): 459-72.

[5] Elie Kedourie, *Democracy and Arab Political Culture* (Washington, D.C.: Washington Institute of Near Eastern Policy, 1992).

countries in the latest global rankings on freedom and democracy provided by 'experts' at the Freedom House. It is questionable if we can evaluate such complex matters by examining snapshots of countries at any one point in time. There is a further problem with the Freedom House rankings: they are subjectively determined. Concerned about the biases this might introduce, the UNDP quickly discontinued their use in their annual *Human Development Report* after using them once.

The cultural determinism of Freedom House is on proud display in their most recent report. On the one hand, a quick review of the record reveals two waves of democratization, in the 1950s and 1990s, which point towards powerful international forces regulating these movements. The first wave accompanied the post-War dismantling of colonies; the second wave followed the end of the Cold War. If some countries, or block of countries, have not participated in these waves of democratization – or pseudo-democratizations for the most part – this is attributed to cultural flaws. Thus, the latest Freedom House report declares that "the *roots* of freedom and democracy are weakest" in the Middle East (emphasis added).

Nevertheless, let us take a closer look at the latest numbers provided by Freedom House. Their data for 2001 show that only 23 percent of the Islamicate countries have electoral democracies; the comparable numbers are 38 percent for Africa, 62 percent for Asian countries, 70 percent for post-Communist countries in Europe and the CIS, and 91 percent for the Americas. There are some revealing patterns *within* the class of Islamicate countries. Of the 16 Arab countries and six Central Asian Republics, not one is democratic. When we exclude these two groups from the Islamicate countries – about a fifth of world's Islamicate population – the proportion of democracies in the remaining Islamicate countries rises to 47 percent. In some cases, the Freedom House classifications are questionable. If we classify Iran and Malaysia as electoral democracies, the last number would go up to 59 percent, quite comparable to the ratio for Asian countries.

Is there any rationale for excluding the Arab and Central Asian countries from the Islamicate count? In fact there are several. Since the end of the Cold War, Western donors and multilateral institutions have used their financial leverage to encourage democratization in client countries. However, there is one significant exception to this. They have not applied these pressures on Islamicate countries – especially in the Arab world – where democratization is likely to bring the Islamists to power. On the contrary, the Arab despotisms – with the exception of the 'rogue states' – have received political, moral and intelligence support from Western powers in the repression of their mainly Islamist opposition.

There are other factors stacking the odds against democracy in the Arab world. Not the least of them is Israel, a colonial-settler state, increasingly seen by Muslims as the military fist of the United States in Zionist gloves. There is no other conflict in the post-War period, barring South African apartheid, which can match the Israel-Arab conflict in its durability or the way it has warped a whole region. The Israeli presence in the Arab heartland magnified the security imperative of the front-line Arab states, allowing them to build praetorian states with the capacity to suppress all forms of dissent.

In the Arab world, oil has been another negative factor. Of the sixteen Arab countries, nine are oil rich, and all but three of them have quite small indigenous populations. Their oil revenues and small populations have allowed most of these countries to exempt their citizens from paying taxes. That is one more strike against democracy: a citizenry that pays no taxes lacks the moral authority to demand representation.

In addition, eight Arab countries are monarchies, and six of them are oil-rich. The British created these oil monarchies, or – in the case of Saudi Arabia and Oman – supported and shored them through difficult times. Since the Second World War, these countries passed under the hegemony of the United States, which has worked through monarchies and dictatorships in the region.

The six Islamicate countries in Central Asia are former members of the defunct Soviet Union. Upon gaining independence, they have been ruled by former communist bosses backed by Moscow. Russia maintains a military presence in these countries, or has strong ties to their military, with the intent of sealing their southern borders against Islamist influence from Iran and Afghanistan. Russia is playing the same role in this region – opposing democratization – that the United States has played in the Arab world.

A Problem for the United States

If Islamicate societies are 'normal', why are they still a problem for the United States?

This problem is born of tensions between a great power, the United States, and a historical adversary, the Islamicate world. The United States enters into this contest with its vast power, Christian evangelism, the constraints of domestic lobbies, energy needs, and a vision of itself as a civilizing force. Islam enters the stage as a fractured, wounded civilization, humiliated by two centuries of Western domination, divided into ineffectual political units, without a core state, rich in oil resources it does not control, with a colonial settler state planted in its heartland that daily adds insults to its injuries. It appears that history has produced an explosive dialectic.

In its most recent convulsion, this dialectic has produced a decentralized, secretive and violent Islamist enemy that, unable to strike at its domestic tormentors, has decided to attack the United States, the most visible protagonist of the corrupt and repressive Islamicate regimes. Having destroyed their only safe haven in Afghanistan, and convinced that the Islamists who intend to perpetrate terror are still lurking in the shadows, the United States desperately searches for appropriate, accessible Islamicate targets.

The camp of the warriors offers easy targets to the United States in this unfolding dialectic. "It's the Islamic world, stupid. Just get rolling and take it out." In the present climate, this temptation will be hard to resist. It will be hard to resist because 9-11, with help from neoconservative commentators, has roused America's old penchant for evangelism, messianism and civilizing mission. If naively, Americans are also convinced of their overwhelming power to inflict damage without taking any losses.

Americans might perhaps take a leaf from Israel, its alter ego in the Middle East. Israel has long enjoyed incomparable military superiority over the Palestinians. It can rain down terror on the Palestinians, as it has for the past 56 years. However, Israel's unmatched military power has not brought it any closer to security or peace. In this contest, the greater responsibility for restraint rests upon the United States. It is the greatest power on earth, possessing greater degrees of freedom than the beleaguered Islamists do. In addition, American power is vested in the hands of Ivy League graduates, realists, sophisticates, men and women deeply acquainted with the modern world, who possess an understanding of the world that the extremist Islamists sorely lack. In this delicate hour, we must pray that the United States will act with restraint, will wield its power with responsibility, and that it will show the world that it is not only a great country, the greatest in the world: it also cares for civilized values.

CHAPTER THREE[1]

A Clash of Civilizations? Nonsense

"O mankind! Lo! We have created you male and female, and have made you nations and tribes that ye may know one another."

Qur'ān: 49:13

March, 2002

Every system of social inequalities conceived in violence must maintain itself by less violent means if it is to endure. Once they are in place, the inequalities must be preserved by social constructs that obscure the mechanisms that reproduce them. In the medieval past, religion formed a central component of such social constructs, but in modern capitalist economies, this task falls to the social sciences. At its highest levels – in the universities, think tanks and the media – the social science orthodoxy occupies a more central place in society than the priestly class ever did. In modern societies, the ideological task has grown more demanding, since the subordinate classes are better educated, better connected with each other, and, in democracies, they could overthrow the system with a vote.

These remarks create an appropriate context for examining Samuel Huntington's thesis of the "clash of civilizations," first offered in

[1] This paper first appeared in *The Journal of the Historical Society* 2, 3-4 (Summer/Fall 2002): 379-96.

an essay and later, following its grand reception, developed into a sizeable book.[2] Huntington's thesis serves to obfuscate the global system of inequalities in power, technology and income that has divided the world into a Core and Periphery – rich and poor countries – for more than two hundred years. The immense popularity of the Huntington thesis among Western intellectuals and policy pundits suggests that it is indeed fulfilling an important ideological function.[3]

The Thesis Dissected

Huntington's thesis of a new era in global politics dominated by a "clash of civilizations" – starting in the 1990s – is embedded in a historiography of global conflicts that is breath-taking in its simplicity.[4] In the first period of human history, starting from the earliest times down to 1500 CE, "contacts between civilizations were intermittent or nonexistent."[5] This conception of minimal contacts, at least among civilizations in the Eastern hemisphere, has no basis in reality; the history of mankind since quite early times has been one of nearly continuous contacts – via trade, migrations, wars and transmission of diseases – amongst all major civilizations in the eastern hemisphere. Even the Greeks understood this quite well; they visualized the world as an *oikoumenikos* that included all the peoples

---

2 Samuel P. Huntington, "The Clash of Civilizations?" *Foreign Affairs* 72, 3 (1993): 22-49; and *The Clash of Civilizations: Remaking of world order* (New York: Simon and Schuster: 1997). Senghaas (1998: 127) notes that the "title of the article included a question mark, whether seriously or rhetorically intended. In the subsequent book, the clash of civilizations, however, became the very definition of the new order of world policy in the 21st century. No question mark any more!" Dieter Senghaas, "A Clash of Civilizations: An Idée Fixe?" *Journal of Peace Research* 35, 1 (January 1998): 127-32.

3 A quick search in google.com, showed 12,600 citations, which included both "Samuel Huntington" and "clash of civilizations."

4 Huntington (1997): 20, 21 and 28.

5 Huntington (1997): 21.

in the inhabited parts of the earth. In Huntington's scheme, this period of isolation is followed by a "multipolar international system," extending from 1500 to 1945 and defined by interaction, competition, wars between Western states, and wars waged by the West against other civilizations. Once again, at the global level, it would appear that the central phenomenon of this period was the rise, expansion and global dominance of capitalism, a set of violent processes, which divided the world into a dominant Core and a subjugated Periphery. The most enduring – and the most deadly – conflicts during this period occurred between the Core and Periphery.

In Huntington's analysis, the end of the Second World War heralded a new period in global politics, the Cold War, dominated by the clash of ideologies between "mostly wealthy" societies, led by the United States, and a group of "somewhat poorer" communist societies led by the Soviet Union. Once again, the attempt at obfuscation should be obvious. First, the communist countries were not "somewhat" but significantly poorer than the developed countries. A substantial and growing gap divided the communist countries of Eastern Europe from the developed countries; and the Asian communist countries lagged by a still greater margin. More importantly, we must see the clash of ideologies during the Cold War for what it was: a clash between the interests of the Core and the Periphery. The Cold War marked a new phase in an old conflict. It was a clash between the Core and a *segment* of the Periphery, which had broken away from the global capitalist system. Similarly, and contrary to Huntington's claims, the end of the Cold War did not change the fundamental reality of a world divided between the Core and the Periphery. It only terminated the socialist development of a recalcitrant segment of the Periphery, and reintegrated it into the global capitalist system. The post-Cold War period also led to the dismantling of developmental states in most Third World countries. If the post-War era marks a new phase in global capitalism, this stems from a new unity in the ranks of the Core countries, which has given them a degree of control over global economic arrangements they have never exercised before. It was during this period that the Core countries created a world government of sorts, in the guise of IMF, World Bank and WTO. Since the end of the Cold War, this triad has succeeded in squeezing the whole world into a straightjacket, designed by and for the advantage of the Core countries.

Huntington summarily dismisses conflicts between the rich and poor countries. Such conflicts are unlikely because the poor countries "lack the political unity, economic power, and military capability to challenge the rich countries."[6] Ironically, this contradicts Huntington's own thesis of the "clash of civilizations" which warns of clashes between the West, on one side, and Islam and China, both of which would easily qualify as poor countries.[7] Huntington's position runs into a variety of other problems. He asserts that poor countries do not pose a threat because they "lack political unity" and "military capability." Why, then, is Huntington so obsessed about a "clash of civilizations" between the West and an Islamicate world that is fragmented into some 50 countries, nearly all quite poor? Moreover, China and India, two still poor countries, each with a population greater than that of the entire West, already constitute a significant and growing economic challenge to the West. Finally, the United States now worries a great deal about the ability of some small *and* poor countries – what it calls "rogue states" – to threaten

---

[6] Huntington (1997): 32-33.

[7] Even after decades of rapid growth, China's per capita income in US dollars – for this is what matters when measuring purchasing power on world markets – was $ 780 in 1999, compared to $ 30,600 for the United States. On an average, the Islamicate countries had lower per capita incomes than China. World Bank, *World Development Report, 2000/2001* (NY: Oxford University Press, 2001): 274-5.

its interests and security. Indeed, the Pentagon now invokes threats from these "rogue states" to justify the large appropriations on the nuclear defense shield.

A closer examination of the "civilizations" in Huntington's "clash of civilizations" reveals that this is mostly a clash of races.[8] Although Huntington does not explain what defines a civilization, what lies at its core, or how it preserves this core over time, he is quite clear about its correlates. People define their identity in terms of characteristics such as ancestry, religion, language, values and institutions.[9] However, it is "ancestry" (alternatively, "blood" and "race") that dominates all other characteristics. We can identify a dominant "race" for all but one of the civilizations on Huntington's list: the Western (Germanic), Orthodox (Slavic), Latin American (mostly Mestizo), Sinic (yellow), Japanese (Japanese), African (black), Indian (brown) and the Caribbean (black). Islamicate civilization is the one exception. On the other hand, the correlation between civilization and religion is quite a bit weaker. The Western, Orthodox, Caribbean and Latin American civilizations are *all* Christian; but the Japanese and Sinic civilizations are not defined by *any* religion, as we commonly understand the term.

An examination of the empirical relation between civilizations and states creates a different kind of problem for the Huntington thesis. Of the six major civilizations – the Western, Orthodox, Islamicate, Indian, Sinic, and Japanese – the last three are identical or nearly identical with a state. In other words, India, China and Japan are civilizations *and* states. In addition, two core states – the United States and Russia – contain a third and a half of the total populations of the civilizations to which they belong, leading some to treat these

---

[8] Senghaas (1998: 127-8) remarks that although "Huntington places civilizations at the center of attention, very little can be learned about them."

[9] Huntington (1997): 21, 42, 126.

countries as synonymous with the Western and Orthodox civilizations. In the presence of such strong overlaps between civilizations and states, one could easily construe an inter-state conflict over interests – say, between the United States and China, or China and Russia – as a clash of civilizations.

Are clashes between civilizations inevitable? According to Huntington, these conflicts have deep roots in human psyche. People define themselves by identifying with "cultural groups: tribes, ethnic groups, religious communities, nations, and, at the broadest level, civilizations." We deepen our identity by differentiating "our" group from other groups. "We know who we are only when we know who we are not and often *only* when we know whom we are against (emphasis added)."[10] Our deeply felt need for identity leads inevitably to cultural conflicts. This two-part thesis lies at the core of Huntington's book. We need to identify with groups, and our group identity battens on hatred of other identities. There are several problems with this thesis. The identification with groups will not always generate conflicts; this will depend on the groups with which we identify. We can define ourselves by identifying with the family, village, tribe, guild, trade union, college, town, profession or club; but we do not necessarily seek to reinforce our attachment to one primary group by hatred of other primary groups. No reason, rooted in our psyche, explains why a commitment to secondary groups, such as nation, race or civilization must supersede our identification with primary groups. Our devotion to secondary groups is socially constructed; we prefer to satisfy our existential need for self-

[10] The quotes in this paragraph are from Huntington (1997): 21. On page 20, Huntington also approvingly quotes this passage from Michael Dibdin's novel, *Dead Lagoon*, "Unless we hate what we are not, we cannot love what we are." In another passage, Huntington (1997: 130) asserts, "For self-definition and motivation people need enemies: competitors in business, rivals in achievement, opponents in politics."

definition by socialization with smaller groups. Similarly, *if* it is human to hate, as Huntington asserts, then surely we would prefer to direct this 'hatred' at our primary rivals in business, politics, sports or the work place.[11]

The obsession with nation, race and civilization assumes prominence only when we view the world from the perspective of modern European history. During the past two thousand years – and perhaps longer – empires have ranked as the most common, enduring and powerful system of governance across the world. More often than not, these empires embraced peoples of diverse ethnicities, religions and even races. In India, home to many rich and well-defined ethnic cultures, ethnic identities only infrequently motivated the politics of state formation.[12] An Indian identity, defined by consciousness of differences from – and hatred of – Others, was never very strong until the British conquest stimulated it. Indians did not trouble to name their continent: the Greeks and, later, the Muslims did.

Huntington attributes civilizational conflicts to cultural differences *per se*, asserting that the conflicts between Islam and the Christian West "flow from the *nature* of the two religions and the civilizations based on them (emphasis added)." In addition, the conflict between these two great civilizations is "fundamental" and "will continue to define their relations in the future as it has defined them for the past fourteen centuries."[13] What then are the core ideas or tendencies within these civilizations, which pit them against each other? Huntington flags several sources of conflicts between Islamicate societies and the West. They take opposite positions on the relation between politics and religion; as monotheisms, Islam and

---

[11] Huntington (1997):130.

[12] The weakness of ethnic consciousness in most of Asia and Africa proved a great advantage to the colonizing Europeans: the colonists could hire Asian and African soldiers to conquer their own peoples.

[13] Huntington (1997): 210-12.

Christianity do no accommodate other gods; both religions claim to be the universal truth; and they compete for converts.

Huntington regards the West and Islam as absolutes: each has a singular and determinate "nature," given at its conception and invariant over time and place. It follows that their differences also are absolute; the two religions are irreconcilable. All this ignores a great deal of history. For instance, the separation between the state and church is a quite recent development that began its career with the founding of United States. In Britain today, the Queen is not only the head of the state, she is also the head of the officially established Anglican Church. On the other hand, the autonomy that Islamicate empires generally offered to protected non-Islamic communities is generally not available under the secular Western democracies. The Ottoman Empire allowed various Christian denominations to administer their religious laws and religious and educational institutions, and even granted them the power to raise taxes to meet their expenses.

The nature of Christian and Islamic claims to universalism and, more importantly, the means employed to achieve them, are historically determined. They have evolved with time, though not always in the direction of greater tolerance. In the medieval past, the Catholic Church viewed Islam as a false religion, which it tried to extirpate by force. For many centuries, this exclusivist vision mobilized waves of Crusaders to wage wars against the Muslims in Spain, the Levant, North Africa and the Balkans. In general, Christian rulers did not tolerate an Islamic presence in territories it conquered from Muslims. In sixteenth century Spain, the Muslims had to choose between conversion and expulsion from their ancestral homes. Moreover, starting in the sixteenth century when the Protestant reformation fractured the religious unity of Western Europe, the Christians waged incessant wars against each other, which, at their height, were far more deadly than any wars fought between Christian Europe and Islamicate societies. In time, however, Christians learned to live with their differences, since the alternative was too costly. In the past two hundred years, the West has not fought any major war that had its roots in religious differences between Catholics and Protestants. Currently, Christianity does not define Western Europe anymore, although it remains a strong element in the identity and politics of the United States. However, Islamicate societies have moved in the opposite direction over the past two centuries, and away from the tolerance mandated by their religion. Faced with the growing marginalization of Islamicate societies, the erosion of their power and institutions, the new Islamic movements have become less tolerant of their own differences as well as other religions. Indeed, the Israeli-Palestinian conflict has increasingly led Muslims to frame their struggle in religious terms, and employ new forms of violence not sanctioned by their religion.

Huntington has more weapons in his armory. "Differences in material interests," he argues, "can be negotiated and often settled by compromise in a way cultural issues cannot."[14] Recent history suggests that the distinction may not be so categorical, since the savage wars the Europeans have fought in modern times were mostly about conflicts of power and material interests. He also overstates the claim that cultural differences are immune to negotiation. The Islamic empires extended a considerable amount of religious and cultural autonomy to non-Islamic communities in their territory. The Ottoman Empire encouraged non-Muslims to organize themselves into *millets*, autonomous communities with the power to regulate their lives according to their own religious laws. In sixteenth century India, the Moghul emperor, Akbar, abolished the *jizya*, an Islamic

---

[14] Huntington (1997): 130.

tax levied on non-Muslims in lieu of military service; he even tried to launch a syncretic religion that would be acceptable to Hindus and Muslims alike. More generally, the Hindus and Muslims in India evolved a common language of discourse – Urdu – a common dress, common forms of address, and a considerable degree of respect for each other's festivals and holy places.

Later, Huntington appears to negate his own thesis – that most conflicts have their source in cultural differences – when he describes the genesis of civilizational conflicts.[15] He argues that these "fault line wars" originate in the usual sources – conflicts over people, territory, resources, and the anarchy of states; religion enters into these conflicts only later as the primary rivals mobilize support among the larger population. "As violence [in fault-line wars] increases, the initial issues at stake tend to get redefined more exclusively as "us" against "them" and group cohesion and commitment are enhanced. Political leaders expand and deepen their appeals to ethnic and religious loyalties, and civilization consciousness strengthens in relation to other identities."[16] This analysis of fault-line wars contradicts Huntington's thesis of the primacy of cultural factors in "civilizational" conflicts.

Finally, Huntington fails to explain the timing of what he thinks were civilizational clashes in the 1990s. He states that "social-economic modernization" caused these clashes.[17] First, modernization created dislocation and alienation, which, in turn, increased the need for more "meaningful identities." Second, as modernization

---

[14] Huntington (1997): 130.

[15] Huntington (1997): 266.

[16] We find a specific example of this in Huntington's (1997: 269) comments on the Bosnian conflict. On the one hand, he claims that this was a fault-line war. On the other hand, he acknowledges that "Bosnian Muslims were highly secular in their outlook, viewed themselves as Europeans, and were the strongest supporters of a multicultural Bosnian society and state."

[17] Huntington (1997): chapters 3 and 4.

increased the points of contact between civilizations, growing awareness of their differences created stronger civilizational identities. Third, economic growth in Asia and population growth in Islamicate societies have revitalized cultural identities in these societies. These explanations fail on several counts. First, there is no evidence that modernization peaked or accelerated across all civilizations in the 1990s. If it did not, it is hard to see how modernization could have caused the clashes of the 1990s. Second, if modernization caused these clashes, they should be emanating from East Asia, not Islamicate societies, as Huntington claims. Third, if population growth causes cultural resurgence, Africa, which has been growing faster than Islamicate societies, should have taken the lead in these clashes. Since population in Latin America too has been growing rapidly since the 1900s, they should have exploded in civilizational clashes much earlier.

The Evidence

There arc two sets of propositions that are central to Huntington's thesis of the clash of civilizations: one relates to such clashes generally, another to claims about the greater propensity of Islamicate societies to get into clashes. Not surprisingly, for a theory that is so flawed in its conception, these propositions do not stand up to the evidence.

The Huntington thesis claims that since 1989 – and before 1945 – two states were more likely to engage in wars if they belong to different civilizations; it was only during the Cold War, between 1945 and 1989, that the competition between two rival ideologies, capitalism and communism, suppressed this propensity. Huntington devotes 367 pages to developing this thesis, but the supporting evidence remains selective and mostly anecdotal. Did he really believe that his thesis about clashes would persuade by its intuition, rooted, as it is, in the existential need for cultural identity, drawing sustenance from a steady diet of loathing for other peoples? Perhaps, he knew all along that ideologies succeed by appealing to interests, not evidence.

Although his thesis of a "clash of civilizations" after 1989 lends itself to quantification, Huntington does not exploit this possibility.[18] He offers one statistic on ethnic conflicts, which shows that slightly less than half of such conflicts in 1993 involved groups from different civilizations, and it is not very helpful. If he wishes to establish a break in the pattern of conflicts after 1989, he needs to compare the trends before and after this date. Jonathan Fox has undertaken such a comparison, and his findings contradict Huntington's thesis.[19] He observed a modest *decline* in inter-civilization conflicts – compared to conflicts within the boundaries of a civilization – as we move from the Cold War (1945-1989) to the post-Cold War period (1990-1998).

Alternatively, we might test Huntington's thesis about the clash of civilizations by exploring if the probability of conflicts rises with cultural differences in the post-Cold War period. For this, we would need to control for other factors that affect conflicts. In their study of international conflicts, Henderson and Tucker identify three such factors, in addition to differences in civilization: distance between the countries, the presence of democracy, and an index of power capabilities.[20] Once Henderson and Tucker introduce controls for these influences, they find that cultural factors had no visible impact

---

[18] Huntington (1997): 37.

[19] Jonathan Fox, "Two Civilizations and Ethnic Conflict: Islam and the West," *Journal of Peace Research* 38, 4 (2000): 459-72.

[20] Errol A. Henderson and Richard Tucker, "Clear and Present Strangers: The Clash of Civilizations and International Conflict," *International Studies Quarterly* 45 (2001): 317-38. We might add another factor to this list: the length of borders a country shares with countries from a different civilization.

on the probability of wars during the post-Cold War years. Again, Huntington's thesis of the clash of civilizations falls short.

Although the period before 1945 offers fertile ground for testing his thesis, Huntington shows little interest in this period. In his 1993 paper, however, he claims that over the centuries "differences among civilizations have generated the most prolonged and the most violent conflicts."[21] Again, history does not support this conclusion. Of 18 major wars fought by great powers between 1600 and 1945, only six involved states from two or more civilizations, and the deadliest, which caused millions of deaths, were fought among Western states.[22] When Henderson and Tucker examined international wars between 1816 and 1945, with controls for other influences, they found that the probability of conflicts between two states was *greater* if they belonged to the *same* civilization – the opposite of what Huntington predicts.

Huntington asserts that culture, not geography, forms the basis of cooperation among nations. In the military field, he cites the example of NATO as the most successful example of such cooperation.[23] He forgets that NATO is a vestige of the Cold War. It was created to defeat the Soviet Union, and not a few have questioned its utility in the post-Cold War era. More significantly, during the 35 years that preceded its formation, the countries that are at the core of NATO had fought the two bloodiest wars in human history. In the same spirit, Huntington offers the European Union as the greatest success in economic cooperation, which he attributes to the common culture

---

[21] Huntington (1993): 25.

[22] These data are from Jack Levy, *War in the Modern Great Power System, 1495-1975* (Lexington, KY: University Press of Kentucky, 1983), quoted in Charles Tilly, *Coercion, Capital and European States, 990-1990* (Oxford: Basil Blackwell, 1990): 165-66. Major wars are those with at least 100,000 battle-deaths.

[23] Huntington (1997): 130-35.

of its members.[24] While a connection may exist between culture and economic cooperation, Huntington's conclusion fails on several counts. First, this cooperation was motivated from its outset by the threat of economic competition from the United States, another *Western* country, and no one has proposed turning the European Union into an Atlantic Union. The success of economic cooperation has better prospects among neighbors at similarly advanced levels of development than among those who share only a common culture. In the fifty years before the Second World War, Europeans were not clamoring for the creation of a customs union; even after 1950, the Europeans proceeded slowly, taking nearly fifty years, to weld their disparate economies into an economic union. Further complicating matters, the European Union has begun to open its doors to several countries in Eastern Europe, with Orthodox majorities.

Other examples of organizations that span several civilizations receive little attention or respect in Huntington's analysis. Thus, he sneeringly dismisses ASEAN as "an example of the limits" of such organizations,[25] and yet ASEAN has enjoyed demonstrable success over its relatively short existence. Founded in 1967 to promote regional security, ASEAN moved towards the creation of a customs union in 1977 and a free-trade area in 1992. In recent years, ASEAN has expanded its membership from the original five to ten countries, and is already very close to achieving its goal of creating a free-trade area. In November 2001, ASEAN and China signed an agreement to create the world's largest free-trade area within 10 years.[26] Outside of the developed countries, the creation of a free-trade area has moved fastest amongst countries with diverse cultures.

Now consider the accusations about the "bloody borders" of

---

[24] Huntington (1997): 131.
[25] Huntington (1997): 132.
[26] http://www.forbes.com/newswire/2001/11/06/rtr415466.html

Islamicate societies. Huntington asserts that Muslims "have problems living peaceably with their neighbors," and "in the 1990s they have been far more involved in intergroup violence than the people of any other civilization."[27] In support, he presents various bits of data from 1992-1994 purporting to show that Muslims were disproportionately engaged in wars with other civilizations. A more careful examination of the data tells a different story. Surveying ethnic conflicts, Fox found that Islamicate societies were involved in 23.2 percent of all inter-civilizational conflicts between 1945 and 1989, and 24.7 percent of these conflicts during 1990 to 1998.[28] First, we do not observe a dramatic rise in the Islamicate world's share of conflicts since the end of the Cold War. Second, the Islamicate world's share of conflicts is quite close to their share of the world population.

Islamicate societies appear to have bloodier borders because they have a proportionately larger share of inter-civilizational borders. The Islamicate world stretches from Senegal, Morocco and Bosnia in the West to Sinjiang, Indonesia and Mindanao in the East. This geographic sweep across the Afro-Eurasian landmass brings Islamicate societies into contact – both close and extensive – with the African, Western, Orthodox, Hindu and Buddhist civilizations. If we add up all these borders – inter-country and intra-country borders – the share of Islamicate societies might well exceed the combined share of all other civilizations. All this should help to place observations about Islam's "bloody borders" in a less prejudicial perspective.

September 11 and the "Clash"

September 11 will remain a day inscribed in infamy. But does it mark the first strike in a clash of civilizations – predicted by our sage political scientist?

---

[27] Huntington (1997): 256-57.
[28] Fox (2001): 464.

Samuel Huntington prevaricates, but he appears to stick to his guns. In an interview, he declared that the attacks "were not a clash of civilizations but a blow by a fanatical group on civilized societies in general."[29] So, it is *not* an attack on United States, or its policies, but an attack on "civilized societies in general," often a synonym for the West. Other voices were more forthright, declaring that this *is* a clash of civilizations.[30] Should we accept this reading of September 11 as an attack on the West, and part of an unfolding war between the West and Islamicate societies? In my judgement, even the most elementary facts show that this thesis is indefensible.

The events of September 11 mark an escalation in attacks of a similar nature. The history of such attacks – starting with the 1983 attacks on US interests in Lebanon, winding through more attacks on US embassies, US military facilities, US officials and US citizens in Kuwait, Saudi Arabia, Yemen, Britain, Germany, Tanzania and Kenya, and leading up to their culmination in the attacks of September 11 – reveals two unpleasant facts. In nearly all cases, the target of these attacks was unmistakably the United States.[31] In nearly every case, these attacks were carried out by Arabs, on Arab soil at first, then in non-Arab countries, and, eventually, to attacks on US soil. In the 1980s, the attackers were mostly Lebanese and Palestinians. Later, Egyptians and Saudis joined them.

This history establishes that the attackers were not waging war against "all civilized societies in general", but against *one* in

---

[29] John Vinocur, "Taboos Are Put to Test in West's Views of Islam," *International Herald Tribune* (October 9, 2001). www.iht.com/ articles/35046.html (accessed January 1, 2002). This is also the official position of the government of the United States.

[30] Robert S. Wistrich, "It Is a Clash of Civilizations," *Jerusalem Post* (October 19, 2001); and March Erikson, "It Is a "Clash of Civilizations"," *Asia Times* (November 28, 2001).

[31] John Moore, "The Evolution of Islamic Terrorism: An Overview." www.pbc. org.wgbh/pages/frontline/shows/target/etc/modern.html (accessed November 11, 2001).

particular – the United States – with less than one-third of the population of the West. They were not waging war against the West, or the freedom, democracy and pluralism of Western societies. The attacks were primarily aimed at military and official targets, with the Lockerbie crash and the two attacks on WTC as notable exceptions. Equally important, nearly all the attackers were of Arab ethnicity. We must reject Huntington's reading of the attacks of September 11, which, like previous attacks, had a specific target – the United States. Even if we regard the attackers as representative of all Arab societies – a questionable assumption – this only pits one-sixth of Islamdom against less than one-third of the West. This is not exactly a clash between two civilizations. Instead, it points to deep tensions between a specific country, the United States, and the Arab world – and to US policies in the Middle East, which have mediated the relations between the two.

Concluding Remarks

Why has the Huntington thesis dominated public discourse in the West despite its weak theoretical foundations, the lack of empirical support for its most important predictions, and its frequent descent to espousal of hatred as the necessary basis of cultural identity?

This question may be answered with a story from Mulla Nasruddin, an enigmatic character in the Sufi folklore of the Islamicate world, at once funny and unpredictable, but always revealing. On one occasion, the Mulla borrowed a large cooking pot from his neighbor. When he returned the pot a few days later, he placed a smaller pot inside the larger one. His neighbor reminded the Mulla that he had borrowed only one pot, to which the Mulla replied, "Oh that's a baby pot. While your pot was with me, it gave birth to a baby." The neighbor asked no further questions. Several days later, the Mulla borrowed another pot from the same neighbor. This time, however, he chose not to return it. When the neighbor asked for his pot, the Mulla explained that he could not have it – the pot had died. Visibly upset, the neighbor expostulated, "Do you take me for a fool. Pots don't die." The Mulla answered: "If it could have a baby, why can't it die?"

This story illuminates an important aspect of the nature of ideologies; although there are other ways of reading the Mulla's antics. Our acceptance of narratives, even quite ridiculous ones, depends on how well they serve our interests – individual and collective ones. Not a few of the stories social scientists have constructed about race, climate, culture, civilizations, free markets and free trade, although thickly interwoven with logic, rhetoric, mathematics and statistics, are equally ridiculous, if only they could be seen in their true colors. Nevertheless, they endure so long as they serve powerful interests. They endure because these powerful interests can employ a legion of scholars who willingly – though often unwittingly – trade the prestige of their scholarship for a good job, good pay, and the accolades of their bosses.

Huntington's "clash" conjures up images of Islamic vandals attacking cherished Western values: freedom, democracy and secularism. It tells us, we are in a conflict with an age-old adversary: it is *our* Crusade against *their* Jihad. Once we hijack these images, we succeed in obscuring the real issues, about the system of global inequities and the structural violence it has perpetrated daily, routinely, for more than two hundred years. It obscures questions about America's foreign policy in the Middle East and about the 'blowback' from that policy. It mobilizes the approval ratings, which then allow us to deal with the 'blowback' with more violence. If the Huntington thesis prevails, the twenty-first century will return the West and Islamdom to the twelfth century, when they fought wars in the name of religion. Only this time it is likely to by much worse for both antagonists.

CHAPTER FOUR[1]

Bernard Lewis: Scholarship or Sophistry?

"Confound not truth with falsehood, nor knowingly conceal the truth."

Qur'ān: 2:42

February 4, 2002

It would appear from the fulsome praise heaped by mainstream reviewers on Bernard Lewis's most recent and well-timed book, *What Went Wrong? Western Impact and Middle Eastern Response*, that the demand for Orientalism has reached a new peak.[2] America's search for new enemies that began soon after the end of the Cold War very quickly resurrected the ghost of an old though now decrepit 'enemy,' Islamdom. Slowly but surely, this revived the sagging fortunes of Orientalism, so that it speaks again with the treble voice of authority.

The mainstream reviewers describe Bernard Lewis as "the doyen of Middle Eastern studies," the "father" of Islamic studies,

[1] This paper first appeared in *Studies in Contemporary Islam* 4, 1 (Spring 2002): 53-80.

[2] Bernard Lewis, *What Went Wrong? Western Impact and Middle Eastern Response* (Oxford: Oxford University Press, 2002).

"arguably the West's most distinguished scholar on the Middle East," and "a Sage for the Age."[3] Lewis is still the reigning monarch of Orientalism, as he was some twenty-five years ago, when Edward Said dissected and exposed the intentions, modalities, deceptions, and imperialist connections of this ideological enterprise.[4] This Orientalist tiger has not changed his stripes over the fifty-odd years that he has been honing his predatory skills. Now at the end of his long career – only coincidentally, also the peak – he presents the summation, the quintessence of his scholarship and wisdom on Islam and the Middle East, gathered, compressed in the pages of this slim book that sets out to explain what went wrong with Islamicate history, and that has so mesmerized reviewers on the right.

Who Is Bernard Lewis?

We will return to the book in a moment, but before that, we need to step back some twenty-five years and examine how Edward Said, in *Orientalism*, has described this Orientalist tiger's stripes and his cunning ploys at concealment. Edward Said gets to the nub of Lewis's Orientalist project when he writes that his "work purports to be liberal objective scholarship but is in reality very close to being propaganda *against* his subject material." Lewis's work is "aggressively ideological." He has dedicated his entire career, spanning more than five decades, to a "project to debunk, to whittle down, and to discredit the Arabs and Islam." Said writes: "The core of Lewis's ideology about Islam is that it never changes, and his whole mission is

---

[3] The first three quotes are from the *New York Times*, the *National Review*, and *Newsweek*, respectively, and are showcased on the Oxford University Press website: www.oup-usa.org/isbn/0195144201.html. The last quote is the title of an article from *Jewsweek*, 4 September 2002; available at www.jewsweek.com/israel/ 092.htm.

[4] Edward Said, *Orientalism* (New York: Vintage Books, 1978).

to inform conservative segments of the Jewish reading public, and anyone else who cares to listen, that any political, historical, and scholarly account of Muslims must begin and end with the fact that Muslims are Muslims."

Although Lewis's objectives are ominous, his methods are subtle; he prefers to work "by suggestion and insinuation." In order to disarm his readers, he delivers frequent "sermons on the objectivity, the fairness, the impartiality of a real historian." However, this is only a cover, a camouflage, for his political propaganda. Once he is seated on his high Orientalist perch, he goes about cleverly insinuating how Islam is deficient in and opposed to universal values, which, of course, always originate in the West. It is because of this defect in their values that Arabs have trouble accepting a democratic Israel; it is always "democratic" Israel. Lewis can write "objectively" about the Arab's "ingrained" opposition to Israel without ever telling his readers that Israel is an imperialist creation, a racist and expansionist colonial-settler state that was founded on terror, wars and ethnic cleansing. Lewis's work on Islam represents the "culmination of Orientalism as a dogma that not only degrades its subject matter but also blinds its practitioners."[5]

Lewis's scholarly mask slips off rather abruptly when he appears on television, a feat that he accomplishes with predictable regularity. Once he is on the air, his polemical self, the Orientalist crouching tiger, takes over, all his sermons about objectivity forgotten, and then he does not shrink from displaying his sneering contempt for the Arabs and Muslims more generally, his blind partisanship for Israel, or his bristling hostility toward Iran. One recent example will suffice here. In a PBS interview broadcast on 16 April 2002, hosted by Charlie Rose, he offered this gem: "Asking Arafat to give up terror-

---

[5] All the quotes in this and the preceding paragraph are from Said (1978): 314-320.

ism would be like asking Tiger to give up golf."[6] That is a statement whose malicious intent and vindictive meanness might have been excusable if it came from an Israeli official deflecting attention from the brutal Israeli Occupation of Palestinian lands.

After this background check, do we really want to hear from this "sage" about "what went wrong" with Islamicate societies? Why, after nearly a thousand years of expansive power and world leadership in many branches of the arts and sciences, they began to lose their élan, their military advantage, and their creativity, and, starting in the nineteenth century, capitulated to their historical adversary, the West? Although Islamicate societies have regained their political independence, why has their economic and cultural decline proved so difficult to reverse? Yet, although our stomachs turn at the prospect, we must sample the gruel Lewis offers, taste it, and analyze it, if only to identify the toxins that it contains and that have poisoned far too many Western minds for more than fifty years.

Where Is the Context?

What went wrong with the Islamic societies? When our "doyen" of Middle Eastern studies asks this question – and right after the attacks of 11 September too – it is hard not to notice that this manner of framing the problem of the eclipse of Islamicate societies by the West is loaded with biases, value judgments and preconceptions; it also contains its own answer. There are two sets of "wrongs" in *What Went Wrong*? The first consists of "wrongs," deviations from what is just and good, that we confront in *contemporary* Islamicate societies. Lewis undoubtedly has in mind a whole slew of problems, including the political, economic and cultural failings of the Islamicate world.

---

6 Jay Nordlinger, "Arafat and Tiger, Nimoy and Shatner, Reagan and Wayne, &c.," *National Review Online*, 2 May 2002; available at www.nationalreview.com/impromptus/ impromptus050202.asp.

In addition, this question seeks to discover deeper "wrongs," deviations from what is just and good that are prior to and lie at the root of the present "wrongs." Lewis is concerned primarily with this second set of "wrongs" that have derailed Islamicate history.

The first problem one encounters in Lewis's narrative of Middle Eastern decline is the absence of a context. He never locates the problem of Islamicate backwardness in its global setting, where backwardness has been endemic to all societies in the Periphery, including the Indian, Chinese, Islamicate, African and Latin American. Instead, he seeks to create the impression that only Islamicate societies have failed to catch up with the West, that this is a specifically Islamic failure. This Middle Eastern focus reveals to all but the blinkered the *mala fides* of *What Went Wrong?* Lewis cannot deceive us with pious claims that a historian's "loyalties may well influence his choice of subject of research; they should not influence his treatment of it."[7] His exclusive focus on the decline of the Middle East is not legitimate precisely because it is designed to – and it unavoidably must – "influence his treatment of it."

Once Western Europe began to make the transition from a feudal-agrarian to a capitalist-industrial base, starting in the sixteenth century, the millennial balance of power among the world's major civilizations began to shift inexorably in favor of Western Europe. A feudal-agrarian society could not match the social power of societies with a capitalist-industrial base. Increasingly, the latter were organized into nation states, whose mercantilist pursuit of power constantly pushed them to augment their military power through industrial strength. To this end, they stimulated the development of a national bourgeoisie; promoted innovations in statecraft, bureaucracy, and civil and military technology; and took advantage of the

---

[7] Bernard Lewis, *Islam in History: Ideas, Men and Events in the Middle East* (London: Alcove Press, 1973): 65.

growing knowledge of markets to design more effective industrial policies. In addition, as the nation states forged a national consciousness, they became better at commanding national resources in the pursuit of nationalist goals. Altogether, these developments made it difficult for non-Western societies to rise up to the challenge offered by Western power. It was unlikely that non-Western societies could simultaneously alter the foundations of their societies while fending off military attacks from Western states. Even as these feudal-agrarian societies sought to reorganize their economies and institutions, Western onslaughts against them escalated, and this made their reorganization increasingly difficult. It is scarcely surprising that the growing asymmetry between the two sides eventually led to the eclipse, decline or subjugation of nearly *all* non-Western societies.

Unlike Lewis, who studiously avoids any reference to this new disequalizing dynamic, another Western scholar of Islam – not driven by a compulsion "to debunk, to whittle down, and to discredit the Arabs and Islam" – understood this tendency quite well. I am referring here to Marshall Hodgson, whose *The Venture of Islam* shows a deep and, for its time, rare understanding of the interconnectedness, across space and time, amongst all societies in the Eastern hemisphere. He understood very clearly that the epochal changes underway in parts of Western Europe between 1600 and 1800 were creating an altogether new order based on markets, capital accumulation and technological changes, which acted upon each other to produce cumulative growth. Moreover, this dynamic endowed the most powerful Western states with a degree of social power that no one could resist. Once this "Western Transmutation" got well under way, writes Hodgson, it "could neither be paralleled independently nor be borrowed wholesale. Yet it could not, in most cases, be escaped. The millennial parity of social power broke down, with results that were disastrous everywhere."[8]

Clearly, the absence of any comparative perspective in Lewis's narrative of Middle Eastern decline is a ploy. His objective is to whittle down world history, to reduce it to a primordial contest between two historical adversaries, the West and Islamicate societies. This is historiography in the Crusading mode; it purports to resume the Crusades and carry them to their unfinished conclusion, viz. the extirpation of Islam in the one-time Christian lands of the Middle East. Once Lewis has established his framework, with its exclusive focus on a failing Islamicate civilization, it becomes necessary to cast the narrative of this decay as a uniquely Islamic phenomenon: a failure contained in the essence of Islam. The attacks of 9-11 created a large audience for such narratives in the United States. Lewis was ready to meet this demand. It is as if, all his life he had prepared for this occasion.

If Lewis had an interest in exploring the decline of the Middle East, he would be asking why the new, more dynamic capitalist society had emerged in the West and not in the Middle East, India, China, Italy or Africa. This question would have led him to explore the factors that might explain the rise of Western hegemony. However, Lewis ducks this question altogether. Instead, he makes the growing power of the West the starting point of his narrative and concentrates on demonstrating why the efforts of Islamicate societies to catch up with the West were both too little and too late. In other words, he seeks to explain a *generic* phenomenon – the overthrow of agrarian societies before the rise of a new historical system, based on capital, markets and technological change – as one that is *specific* to

---

[8] Marshall Hodgson, *The Venture of Islam*: *Conscience and History in a World Civilization*, 3 volumes (Chicago: University of Chicago Press, 1974): 200.

Islam and is due to specifically Islamic "wrongs."[9]

Clearly, the Middle Eastern response to the Western challenge was inadequate. The Ottoman Empire, once the most powerful in the Islamicate world, had lost nearly all its European territories by the end of the nineteenth century, and the remnants of its Arab territories were lost during the First World War. Worse still, at the end of the War, the European powers threatened the Turks in their Anatolian heartland, with the British and French occupying Istanbul, the Greeks marching towards Ankara, the Armenians pushing westward in eastern Anatolia, and the French pushing north into Cilicia. Faced with extinction, the Turks mobilized before it was too late; they rallied in Central Anatolia after the War and fought tooth and nail to push back the Bulgarians, Greeks, French and Armenians. In 1922, they succeeded in establishing a new and modern Turkish nation-state over Istanbul, Thrace and all of Anatolia. The Iranians had more luck in preserving their territories, though, like the Ottomans, they too had lost control over their economic policies in the first decades of the nineteenth century.

Nevertheless, in a comparative setting, the Middle East's record of resisting imperialism is not the worst. First, nearly all of South Asia, East and Southeast Asia, and Africa was colonized by the Europeans during the nineteenth century. Only Japan, Thailand, China and Ethiopia avoided direct colonization during this period, though Ethiopia and much of China were colonized during the 1930s. Moreover, given its proximity to Europe, the Middle East came early and directly in the path of European imperial ambitions. It is also the case that Europe's colonial appetite in the Middle East was stimulated by the historical legacy of the region. Not a few thought of the new colonization as the resumption of the Crusade

---

[9] Lewis (2002):151-152.

against old adversaries. Under the circumstances, it is significant that much of this region managed to avoid direct colonization during the nineteenth century.

Uncurious Ottomans

There is even less support for Lewis's charge that Middle Eastern societies responded too slowly to Western threats, especially when we compare their responses to these threats with the record of East Asian societies.[10]

First, consider Lewis's charge that the Muslims showed little curiosity about the West. He attributes this failing to Muslim bigotry that frowned upon contacts with the infidels.[11] This is a curious charge against "a world civilization" that Lewis admits was "polyethnic, multiracial, international, one might even say intercontinental."[12] It also seems strange that the Ottomans, and other Middle Eastern states before them, were quite happy to take their Christian and Jewish subjects into employment – as high officials, diplomats, physicians and bankers – traded with the Europeans, bought arms and borrowed money from them, and yet, somehow, loathed learning anything from

---

[10] Unlike the Islamicate world, China, Korea and, after an early period of openness, Japan, pursued a policy of minimal contacts with Western nations. After 1760, China restricted all foreign trade to one port, Canton, where foreigners were permitted to reside only during the trading season, from October to March. Starting in 1637, Korea banned all contacts with foreigners except the Chinese, a policy that earned it the reputation of the Hermit Kingdom. In the same year, Japan's trading contacts with Western nations were restricted to one annual visit by a Dutch ship to the tiny island of Deshima. China did not open additional ports to foreign trade until after its defeat in the Opium Wars (1840-1842); the Japanese ended their isolation, under American pressure, in 1850; and Korea did not open its doors to Western nations until 1882. William H. McNeill, *The Rise of the West* (Chicago: University of Chicago Press, 1991): 643-648; Jonathan D. Spence, *The Search for Modern China* (New York: W. W. Norton and Co., 1999): 121.

[11] Lewis (2002): chapter 2.

[12] Lewis (2002): 6.

the same 'infidels.' In addition, Muslim philosophers, historians and travelers have left several very valuable accounts of non-Islamic societies. Among others, Al-Biruni's monumental study of India remains without a rival for its encyclopedic coverage, objectivity, and sympathy for its subject. Clearly, Lewis has fallen prey to the Orientalist temptation. When something demands a carefully researched explanation, an understanding of material and social conditions, he prefers to pin it on some cultural propensity of Islamicate societies.

Lewis is little aware how his book is littered with contradictions. If the Muslims were not a little curious about developments in the West, it is odd that the oldest map of the Americas, prepared by a Turkish admiral and cartographer, Piri Reis, in 1513, is also the most accurate map from the sixteenth century.[13] In addition, Muslims were writing accounts of their travels to Europe from an early date. Lewis refers to no fewer than ten such accounts, nearly all of them written by Ottomans, spanning the period from 1665 to 1840. One of them, Ratib Effendi, who was in Vienna from 1791 to 1792, left a report that "ran to 245 manuscript folios, ten times or more than ten times those of his predecessors, and it goes into immense detail, primarily on military matters, but also, to quite a considerable extent, on civil affairs."[14] Diplomatic contacts provide another indicator of the early Ottoman interest and involvement in the affairs of European states. Between 1703 and 1774, the Ottomans signed sixty-eight treaties or agreements

---

[13] Gregory McIntosh, *The Piri Reis Map of Europe* (Athens, GA.: University of Georgia Press, 2000). Lewis (2002: 37) gives the impression that the Ottomans made little use of the Piri Reis map; they deposited the map in the Topkapi Palace in Istanbul, "where it remained, unconsulted and unknown" until it was discovered in 1929. There is no basis for this assertion. In fact, Reis prepared two maps of the world, one in 1513 and another in 1528; besides these he drew many other charts and maps that were assembled into a book, *Kitab-i-Behriye* (Book of the Sea), which was made available in two editions. See Gregory McIntosh, "A Tale of Two Admirals," *Mercator's World: The Magazine of Maps, Atlases, Globes, and Charts* (May-June 2000).

[14] Lewis (2002): 27.

with sovereign, mostly European states.[15] Since each treaty must have involved at least one diplomatic exchange, it would be difficult to accuse the Ottomans of neglecting diplomatic contacts with Europe.

Was there a failure of vision, as Lewis claims, in the Ottoman decision not to challenge Portuguese hegemony in the Indian Ocean in the sixteenth century? Despite some early warnings from elder statesmen, they chose to concentrate their war efforts on acquiring territory in Europe, which they saw as "the principal battleground between Islam and Europe, the rival faiths competing for enlightenment – and mastery – of the world."[16] First, we can scarcely blame the Ottomans for not anticipating that the Portuguese incursion would translate some 250 years later into a broader and more serious European challenge to their power. It is doubtful if this was because the Ottomans lacked the ability to launch an adequate response to a maritime challenge. Departing from their own tradition of land warfare, the Ottomans, starting in the fifteenth century, had built a powerful navy and created a seaborne empire in the eastern Mediterranean, the Black Sea and the Red Sea. If the Ottomans chose to concentrate their resources on land wars in Central Europe rather than challenge Portuguese hegemony in the Indian Ocean, this was not the result of religious zealotry. It reflected the balance of class interests in the Ottoman political structure. In an Empire that had traditionally been land-based, the interests of the landowning classes prevailed against commercial interests that looked to the Indian Ocean for their livelihood. Although the decision not to contest the Portuguese presence in the Indian Ocean in the sixteenth century proved to be fateful, that policy was rational for the Ottomans.[17]

---

[15] Donald Quataert, *The Ottoman Empire, 1700-1922* (Cambridge: Cambridge University Press, 2000): 75.

[16] Lewis (2002): 15.

[17] Andrew C. Hess, "The Evolution of the Ottoman Seabourne Empire in the Age of

A Military Decline?

Several Orientalists – Lewis amongst them[18] – have argued that the military decline of the Ottoman Empire became irreversible after its second failed siege of Vienna in 1683, or perhaps earlier, after its naval defeat at Lepanto in 1571. In an earlier work, Lewis claimed that "the Ottomans found it more and more difficult to keep up with the rapidly advancing Western technological innovations, and in the course of the eighteenth century the Ottoman Empire, itself far ahead of the Islamic world, fell decisively behind Europe in virtually all arts of war."[19]

Jonathan Grant has convincingly questioned this thesis of an early and inexorable decline. The Ottomans occupied the third tier in the hierarchy of military technology, behind innovators and exporters, at the beginning of the fifteenth century; they could reproduce the latest military technology with the help of foreign expertise but they never graduated into export or introduced any significant innovations. The Ottomans succeeded in maintaining this relative position, through two waves of technology diffusion, until the early nineteenth century. However, they failed to keep up with the third wave of technology diffusion, based upon the technology of the industrial revolution, which began in the mid-nineteenth century. The Ottomans fell below their third-tier status only toward the end of the nineteenth century, when they became totally dependent on imported weaponry.[20]

---

the Oceanic Discoveries, 1453-1525," in Felipe Fernández-Armesto, ed., *The Global Opportunity* (Variorum, 1995): 218. It is unlikely that the Ottomans faced any insuperable barrier to the adoption of the new the naval technology; the North Africans managed to do this toward the end of the sixteenth century [Hess (1995): 222].

[18] Lewis (2002): 151.

[19] Bernard Lewis, *The Muslim Discovery of Europe* (New York: W. W. Norton, 1982): 226.

[20] Jonathan Grant, "Rethinking the Ottoman "Decline": Military Technology Diffusion in the Ottoman Empire, Fifteenth to Eighteenth Centuries," *Journal of World History* 10, 1 (1999):179-201.

If we put together the evidence made available by Lewis,[21] it becomes clear that the Ottomans were not slow in recognizing the institutional superiority enjoyed by Europe's military. A debate about the causes of Ottoman weakness began after the Treaty of Carlowitz in 1699, growing more intense over time. A document from the early seventeenth century recognized that "it was no longer sufficient, as in the past, to adopt Western weapons. It was also necessary to adopt Western training, structures, and tactics for their effective use." The Ottomans began to dispatch special envoys to European capitals "with instructions to observe and to learn and, more particularly, to report on anything that might be useful to the Muslim state in coping with its difficulties and confronting its enemies." Several of these envoys wrote reports, occasionally quite extensive and detailed, on their European visits, and these reports had an important impact on thinking in Ottoman circles. The first mathematical school for the military was founded in 1734, and a second one followed in the 1770s.

While the Ottomans generally kept up with advances in military technology, at least into the first decades of the nineteenth century, they took longer to introduce supporting organizational changes. As a result, the first serious attempts at modernizing the army did not begin until the late eighteenth century, during the reign of Selim III, who sought to bypass the problems of reforming the existing military corps by recruiting and training a new European-style army. Although, he had raised a modern army of nearly twenty-five thousand by 1806, he had to abandon his efforts in the face of resistance from the ulama and a Janissary rebellion. He took up this task again in 1826 after disbanding the Janissary corps, and in two years, the new Ottoman army included seventy-five thousand regular troops. Simul-

[21] Lewis (2002): 20, 25-29.

taneously, the Ottomans introduced reforms in the bureaucracy; they also reformed land-tenure policies with the objective of raising revenues.[22] Yet these efforts at modernizing the Ottoman military – quite early by most standards – failed to avert the progressive fragmentation and eventual demise of the Ottoman Empire at the end of World War I. One might join Hodgson in thinking that this was inevitable, that agrarian societies in Asia and Africa could not modernize fast enough in the face of the ever-increasing economic and military power of the modern Western nation-states.[23] Perhaps, this assessment is too fatalistic. Among others, the Russians modernized in time to save their Empire.

A comparison of the Ottoman and Russian experiences at modernization reveals several extraneous factors that undermined the Ottoman initiatives. The Ottoman Empire, which straddled three continents, lacked the compactness that might have made its territories more defensible. In addition, the Ottoman Turks, the ethnic core of the Ottoman Empire, made up less than a third of its population and occupied an even smaller part of its territories. Finally, the nationalist ideas emanating from Europe found fertile ground in the Ottoman Empire, which had organized its religious minorities into autonomous religious communities. Starting in the nineteenth century, the Ottomans faced one nationalist insurrection after another in the Balkans, each backed by one or more European powers, until the last of these territories broke free by the early decades of the twentieth century. In as much as these insurrections

---

[22] Roger Owen, *The Middle East in the World Economy, 1800-1914* (London: I. B. Tauris, 1993): 58, and, J. C. Hurewitz, "The Beginnings of Military Modernization in the Middle East: A Comparative Analysis," *Middle East Journal* 22 (1968): 2:149.

[23] Lewis (2002), of course, argues that the modernization did not go far enough because of fundamental flaws in Islamicate institutions; we will return to this argument.

reduced the revenues of the Empire and diverted its resources to war, they delayed the modernization of the military and economy. Finally, during World War I, the British and the French divested the Empire of all its Arab territories.

The Egyptian program to modernize its military, which began in 1815 under the leadership of Muhammad Ali, was more ambitious and more successful. It was part of an integrated program of modernization and industrial development financed through state ownership of lands, development of new export crops, and state-owned monopolies over the marketing of the major agricultural products. In 1831, Egypt's Europeanized army consisted of one hundred thousand officers and men, and two years later, after conquering Syria, it was penetrating deep into Anatolia when its advance was halted by Russian naval intervention. The major European powers intervened again in 1839 – all of them but the French – to stop the Egyptians from advancing upon Istanbul.[24] They forced the Egyptians to withdraw, give up their acquisitions in Syria and Arabia, reduce their military force to eighteen thousand, and enforce the Anglo-Ottoman Commercial Convention, which required the lowering of tariffs to three percent and the dismantling of all state monopolies.[25] By depriving Egypt of its revenues and dramatically reducing the military's demand for its manufactures, these measures abruptly terminated the career of the earliest and most ambitious program to build a modern, industrial society in the Periphery.

Lewis faults the Ottomans and Egyptians for seeking to build a modern industrial economy. He thinks it odd that these countries "tried to catch up with Europe by building factories, principally to equip and

---

[24] The Egyptian superiority during the Syrian campaigns was quite decisive; they won easy victories even when they were outnumbered two to one. David Ralston, *Importing the European Army* (Chicago: University of Chicago Press, 1990): 89.

[25] Hurewitz (1968): 145-48.

clothe their armies."[26] All too often, the military has provided the markets and the impetus for pushing through a program of early industrialization. In fact, the Ottomans and Egyptians were leading the way. Of course, Lewis thinks that the Ottomans should have been working harder to remedy their cultural deficiencies, especially their less-than-enthusiastic appreciation for European harmonies.

Industrial Failure – But Why?

Lewis declares that the industrialization programs launched by the Ottomans and Egypt "failed, and most of the early factories became derelict."[27] These programs were doomed from the outset because their promoters lacked a proper regard for time, measurement, harmonies, secularism, and women's rights – values that underpin Western industrial success.

We must correct these jaundiced observations. Far from being a failure, the Egyptian "program of industrialization and military expansion," according to Immanuel Wallerstein, "seriously undermined the Ottoman Empire and almost established a powerful state in the Middle East capable eventually of playing a major role in the interstate system."[28] Muhammad Ali's fiscal and economic reforms, between 1805 and 1847, brought about a more than nine fold increase in government revenues.[29] At their height in the 1830s, Egypt's state monopolies had made investments worth $12 million and employed thirty thousand workers in a broad range of industries that included foundries, textiles, paper, chemicals, shipyards, glass-

[26] Lewis (2002): 46-47.
[27] Lewis (2002): 145-148.
[28] Immanuel Wallerstein, *Unthinking Social Science: The Limits of Nineteenth Century Paradigms* (London: Polity Press, 1991): 14.
[29] Helen Anne B. Rivlin, *The Agricultural Policy of Muhammad Ali in Egypt* (Cambridge: Harvard University Press, 1961), 120.

ware, and arsenals.[30] By the early 1830s, Egyptian arsenals and naval yards had acquired the ability to "produce appreciable amounts of warships, guns and munitions," elevating Egypt "to a major regional power."[31] Naturally, these developments in Egypt were raising concerns in British official circles. A report submitted to the British foreign office in 1837 sounded the right note: "A manufacturing country Egypt never can become – or at least for ages."[32] Three years later, when Istanbul was within the grasp of Muhammad Ali's forces, a coalition of European powers intervened to roll back his gains, downsize his military, and dismantle his state monopolies. These measures successfully reversed the Periphery's first industrial revolution.

The Ottoman program of industrialization was similarly constrained by the jealousy of Western powers. Forced by the Unequal Treaties to limit their import tariffs to less than three percent, the Ottomans were unable to protect their manufactures or raise revenues for investments in development projects. In addition, the Anglo-Turkish Commercial Convention of 1839 forced them to dismantle all state monopolies, dealing another blow to their fiscal autonomy. It speaks to the determination of the Ottomans that they sought to launch an industrial revolution despite their adverse fiscal circumstances. In the decade starting in 1841, the Ottomans had set up to the west of Istanbul a complex of state-owned industries that included spinning and weaving mills, a foundry, steam-operated machine works, and a boatyard for the construction of small steamships. In the words of Edward Clark: "In variety as well as in number, in

---

[30] M. Shahid Alam, *Poverty from the Wealth of Nations* (Houndmills: Macmillan, 2000):115

[31] John Dunn, "Egypt's Nineteenth-Century Armaments Industry," *The Journal of Military History* 61 (1997): 2:236.

[32] L. S. Stavrianos, *Global Rift: The Third World Comes of Age* (New York: William Morrow, 1981), 218.

planning, in investment, and in attention given to internal sources of raw materials these manufacturing enterprises far surpassed the scope of all previous efforts and mark this period as unique in Ottoman history."[33] Several foreign observers saw in the Istanbul industrial complex the potential to evolve into "a Turkish Manchester and Leeds, a Turkish Birmingham and Sheffield," all wrapped in one.[34] Similar projects were initiated in several other parts of the Empire. However, once the Crimean War started, the Ottomans were strapped for funds, and they abandoned most of these industrial projects. Thus ended another bold experiment in industrialization, early even by European standards, but whose failure was linked to the loss of Ottoman fiscal sovereignty.

It's in Their Culture

Lewis blames the political, economic and military failures of the Middle East over the past half a millennium on their culture. He identifies a whole slew of problematic cultural traits, but singles out two for special attention: the mixing of religion and politics and the unequal treatment of women, unbelievers and slaves. Moreover, he insists that these are Islamic flaws.

Lewis argues that secularism constitutes a great divide between Islamdom and the West: the West always had it and Islamdom never did. Secularism, as the separation of church and state, "is, in a profound sense, Christian." Its origins go back to Jesus – his injunction to give God *and* Caesar, each, their due – and to the early history of Christianity when, as a persecuted minority, they developed an independent Church with its "own laws and courts, its own hierarchy and chain of authority." The Church is unique, setting Christian

[33] Edward Clark, "The Ottoman Industrial Revolution," *International Journal of Middle East Studies* 5, 1 (1974): 67.
[34] Clark (1974): 68.

Europe apart from anything that went before and from its competitors. In particular, the Muslims never created an "institution corresponding to, or even *remotely* resembling, the Church in Christendom (emphasis added)."[35]

These claims about a secular Christendom and theocratic Islamicate societies are problematic. Lewis rests his case upon two propositions. First, he contrasts the presence of the Church in Christendom against its absence in Islamdom. Second, he works on the presumption that the existence of a Church, a hierarchical religious organization separate from the state, necessarily implies a separation between religion and political authority. For the most part, these claims are contestable.

The absence of an Islamic Church does not mean that Islamicate societies did not develop a separation between religion and the state. Admittedly, there existed a fusion between the state and religion in early Islamdom; the Prophet and the first four Caliphs combined religious and mundane authority in their persons. In addition, most Islamic thinkers have maintained that the ideal Islamic state must be guided by the Qur'ān and the Prophet's Sunnah. The Islamic practice in the centuries following the pious Caliphs, however, departed quite sharply from the canonical model as well as the theory.

In one of his numerous attempts at distortion, Lewis asserts that the Islamic "pietists" retreated into "radical opposition or quietist withdrawal" when they failed to impose "ecclesiastical constraints on political and military authority."[36] This is only part of the picture. Many pietists turned vigorously to scholarship. Independently of state authority and without state funding, they developed the Islamic sciences, which included the Traditions of the Prophet, biographies

[35] Lewis (2002): 96.
[36] Lewis (2002): 99.

of the Prophet and his companions, Arabic grammar, and theology. Most significantly, these pious scholars elaborated several competing systems of Islamic laws – regulating every aspect of individual, social and business life – on the premise that legislative authority was vested in the consensus of the pious scholars or, in the case of Shi'ites, in the rulings of the imams. The state had executive powers but it possessed no legislative authority. In effect, Islamdom had evolved not only separate political and religious institutions, but it detached the legislative function from the state. It was the pious scholars – with their competing schools of jurisprudence – who constituted the informal legislatures of Islamdom, long before these institutions had evolved in Europe.[37]

Lewis's second proposition – that separation between religion and political authority flows from the presence of a Church – is equally dubious. If the Church commands power over people's lives, it becomes a rival of the state. It does not matter if it exercises this power directly – or indirectly, by using the state for its own ends. In time, after Christianity became the official religion of the Roman state, it used the power of the state to eliminate or marginalize all competing religions; it gained the exclusive right to define all religious dogma and rituals; it acquired properties, privileges and exclusive control over education; it expanded its legislative control over different spheres of society. In time, since the Church and state recruited their higher personnel from the same classes, the two developed an identity of class interests. In other words, although the Church and state remained organizationally distinct, each mixed religion and politics.

---

[37] Lapidus writes that since the middle of the tenth century, "Muslim states were fully differentiated political bodies without any intrinsic religious character, though they were officially loyal to Islam and committed to its defense." Ira Lapidus, *A History of Islamic Societies* (Cambridge: Cambridge University Press, 1988): 364.

The adoption of Christianity as its official creed led the Roman state, hitherto tolerant of all religious communities, to inaugurate a regime of growing intolerance toward other religions, and even toward any dissent within Christianity. As Daniel Schowalter says, "By the end of the fourth century, both anti-pagan and anti-Jewish legislation would serve as licenses for the increasing number of acts of vandalism and violent destruction directed against pagan and Jewish places of worship carried out by Christian mobs, often at the instigation of the local clergy."[38] Although the practice of Judaism was not banned, by the end of the fourth century C.E., a variety of decrees prohibited conversion to Judaism, Jewish ownership of non-Jewish slaves, and marriage between Jews and Christians, and Jews were excluded from most imperial offices.[39] In dogma, theology, legislation and practice, the Church and state crafted a regime that suppressed paganism and marginalized all other non-Christian forms of worship.

The modernization of Islamic societies, Lewis insists, has been plagued by another set of cultural barriers – namely, the inferior status of unbelievers, slaves and, especially, women. Not that these groups labored under greater handicaps than their counterparts in Europe, but their unequal status was "sacrosanct" in that they "were seen as part of the structure of Islam, buttressed by revelation, by the precept and practice of the Prophet, and by the classical and scriptural history of the Islamic community." As a result, these three inequalities have endured; they were not challenged even by the radical Islamic movements that arose from time to time to protest social and economic inequalities.[40]

---

[38] Daniel L. Schowalter, "Churches in the Context: The Jesus Movement in the Roman World," in: Michael D. Coogan, ed., *The Oxford History of the Biblical World* (New York: Oxford University Press, 1998): 570.

[39] Schowalter (1998): 582-583.

[40] Lewis (2002): 83-84.

These claims are problematic for several reasons. First, they lack historicity. Implicitly, Lewis' reading of European history inverts the causation between economic development and social equality. He believes that Europeans developed because they *first* created a more egalitarian society, a necessary basis for rapid progress. This shows a curious indifference to chronology. While Europe was establishing global capitalist empires, it was conducting the Inquisition, expelling the Moors and Jews from Spain, waging unending religious wars, burning witches, and conceded few legal rights to women. In addition, the Europeans introduced systems of slavery in the Americas that would be abolished only after the 1860s. In Russia, serfdom remained the basis of the economy at least until the 1860s. The equality Lewis speaks of began to arrive in slow increments at the beginning of the nineteenth century. It was a byproduct of the industrial revolution, not its precursor.

In comparison to Europe, Islamdom did not practice greater inequalities. Having spent more than fifty years studying the history of the Middle East, it is a bit surprising that "the doyen of Middle Eastern studies" is unaware of at least a few challenges to the 'inferior' status of women or unbelievers. In the early centuries, there were at least three groups – the Kharijis, the Qarmatians and the Sufis – that did not accept the legal interpretations of the four traditional schools of Islamic law as sacrosanct. Instead, they looked for inspiration to the Qur'ānic precepts on the moral and spiritual equality of men and women, claiming that the early applications of these precepts were time-bound. The Kharijis and Qarmatians rejected concubinage and child marriage, and the Qarmatians went further in rejecting polygamy and the veil. In a similar spirit, the Sufis welcomed women travelers on the spiritual path, permitting women "to give a central place in their lives to their spiritual vocation."[41] In

[41] Leila Ahmed, *Women and Gender in Islam* (New Haven: Yale University Press, 1992): 66-67.

sixteenth-century India, the Mughal emperor Akbar abolished the *jizyah* (the poll tax imposed by Islamic law on all non-Muslims), banned child marriage, and repealed a law that forced Islam on prisoners of war.[42]

The "most profound single difference" between Islamdom and the West, however, concerns the status of women. In particular, Lewis argues that Islam permits polygamy and concubinage and that the Christian Churches prohibit it.[43] Once again, Lewis is exaggerating the differences. In nearly all societies, not excluding the Western, men of wealth and power have always had access to multiple sexual partners, although within different legal frameworks. Islam gave equal rights to all the free sexual partners of men as well as to their children. The West, driven by a concern for primogeniture, adopted an opposite solution by vesting all the rights in a man's primary sexual partner and her offspring. All the other sexual partners – a man's mistresses – and their children had no legal rights.[44] Arguably, Europe's mistresses may have preferred the advantages of Islamic law.

Lewis's emphasis on polygamy and concubinage might lead one to conclude that these were very common in Islamdom. In fact, both were quite rare outside the highest circles of the ruling class. Among others, this is attested by European visitors to eighteenth-century Aleppo and nineteenth-century Cairo. A study of documents relating to two thousands estates in seventeenth-century Turkey could identify only twenty cases of polygamy. The practice of concubinage was most likely more rare.[45]

---

[42] Ahrar Ahmad, *Islam and Democracy: Text, Traditions, History* (Black Hills State University, Fall 2001, mimeo): 25.

[43] Lewis (2002): 66.

[44] Marshall G. S. Hodgson, "Cultural Patterning in Islamdom and the Occident," in *Rethinking World History*, ed. Edmund Burke III (Cambridge: Cambridge University Press, 1993): 155.

[45] Ahmed (1992): 107-108.

As if this validated his claims about the "striking contrasts" in women's status in Europe and Islamdom, Lewis reports how Muslim visitors were startled to see European men curtsying to women in public places.[46] Once the bowing and curtsying are done, we need to compare the property rights enjoyed by women in Europe and Islamdom, a quite reliable index of the social power of women inside the household and outside. On this score, too, the Muslim woman held the upper hand until quite recently. Unlike her European counterpart, a married Muslim woman could own property, and she enjoyed exclusive rights to income from her property as well as the wages she earned. In Britain, the most advanced country in Europe, married women did not acquire the right to own property until 1882.

Their superior property gave considerable advantages to Muslim women. If she was a woman of independent means, she could initiate a divorce or craft a marriage contract that prevented her husband from taking another wife. Muslim women often engaged in trade, buying and selling property, lending money, or renting out stores. They created *waqfs*, charitable foundations financed by earnings from property, which they also administered. A small number of women distinguished themselves as scholars of the religious sciences. Women in the early nineteenth century attended al-Azhar, the leading university in the Islamic world. Ahmed concludes that Muslim "women were not, after all, the passive creatures, wholly without material resources or legal rights, that the Western world once imagined them to be."[47]

What Went Wrong?

Why have so many Jewish scholars and columnists, in recent decades, taken culturalist positions on the history and conflicts of the

---

[46] Lewis (2002): 65.
[47] Ahmed (1992): 111.

Middle East, blaming the historical difficulties of the region on its religious and cultural heritage?

In happier times, before the Zionists developed a proprietary interest in Palestine, European Jews often took the least bigoted positions in the field of Oriental studies. These pro-Islamic Jews "were among the first who attempted to present Islam to European readers as Muslims themselves see it and to stress, to recognize, and indeed sometimes to romanticize the merits and achievements of Muslim civilization in its great days."[48] At a time when most Orientalists took Muhammad for a scheming imposter, equated Islam with fanaticism, wrote that the Qur'ān was a crude and incoherent text, and declared that the Arabs were incapable of abstract thought, a growing number of Jewish scholars often took opposite positions. They accepted the sincerity of Muhammad's mission, described Arabs as "Jews on horseback," lauded Islam as an evolving faith that was more democratic than other religions, and debunked Orientalist claims about the contrast between a static Islamdom and a dynamic West.[49] It would appear that these Jews were anti-Orientalists long before Edward Said.

There were several motives behind these contrarian positions. Even as the Jews began to enter the European mainstream, starting in the nineteenth century, they were still outsiders, having only recently emerged from the confinement of ghettos, and it would be scarcely surprising if they were seeking to maintain their distinctiveness by emphasizing and identifying with the achievements of another Semitic people, the Arabs. In celebrating Arab civilization, these Jewish scholars were sending a non-too-subtle message that Arabs often

---

[48] Bernard Lewis, "The Pro-Islamic Jews," in: *Islam in History: Ideas, People, and Events in the Middle East* (Chicago: Open Court, 1993): 12.

[49] Martin Kramer, ed., *The Jewish Discovery of Islam* (Tel Aviv: The Moshe Dayan Center for Middle Eastern and African Studies, 1999), 1-48; www.martinkramer.org/ pages/ 899528/index.htm

excelled Europeans in many fields of human endeavor, and that Europe was building upon Islamicate achievements in science and philosophy. In addition, the Jewish scholars' discussions of religious and racial tolerance in Islamdom, toward Jews in particular, may have offered hope that such tolerance was attainable in Europe too. The discussions may also have been an invitation to Europeans to incorporate religious and racial tolerance in their standards of civilization.

Yet this early anti-Orientalism of Jewish scholars would not survive the logic of the Zionist movement. Since the Zionists sought to create a colonial-settler state in Arab Palestine, they understood quite well that this would lead to conflicts with the Palestinians, whom they planned to drive out of their homes, and with the neighboring Arab states who would be forced to respond to the Zionist occupation of the Arab heartland. This could only be achieved if the Zionist state could gain the support of Western powers, and to secure this, the Zionists early offered to become an outpost of Western powers against the Arabs. As the Zionists mobilized support amongst Jewish constituents in the West, it was inevitable that the European Jews' attraction for Islam was not going to endure. In fact, it would be replaced by a bitter contest, one in which the Jews, as junior partners of Western imperialists, would seek to deepen the Orientalist project in the service of the West. Bernard Lewis played a leading part in this Jewish reorientation. Indeed, in the words of one camp-follower, he "came to personify the post-war shift from a sympathetic to a critical posture."[50]

Ironically, this shift occurred when many Orientalists had begun to shed their Christian prejudice against Islam, even making amends for the excesses of their forebears. Another factor aiding this shift

---

[50] Kramer (1999).

toward a less polemical Orientalism was the entry of a growing number of Arabs, both Muslim and Christian, into the field of Middle Eastern studies. The most visible upshot of these divergent trends was a polarization of the field of Middle Eastern studies into two opposing camps.[51] One camp, consisting mostly of Christians and Muslims, has sought to bring greater objectivity to their study of Islam and Islamicate societies. They seek to locate Islamicate societies in their historical context, arguing that Islamicate responses to Western challenges have been diverse and evolving over time: they do not derive from an innate hostility to the West or some unchanging Islamic mindset. The second camp, led mostly by Jews, has reverted to Orientalism's original mission of subordinating knowledge to Western power, now filtered through the prism of Zionist interests. This Zionist Orientalism has assiduously sought to paint Islam and Islamicate societies as innately hostile to the West, modernism, democracy, tolerance, scientific advance and women's rights.

This Zionist camp has been led for more than fifty years by Bernard Lewis, who has enjoyed an intimate relationship with power that would be the envy of the most distinguished Orientalists of an earlier generation. He has been strongly supported by a contingent of able lieutenants, whose ranks have included the likes of Elie Kedourie, David Pryce-Jones, Raphael Patai, Bat Ye'or, Daniel Pipes and Martin Kramer. There are many foot soldiers, too, who have provided distinguished service to this new Orientalism. And no compendium of these foot soldiers would be complete without the names of Thomas Friedman, Martin Peretz, Norman Podhoretz, Charles Krauthammer, William Kristol and Judith Miller.

---

[51] For a recent evaluation of the conflict between the two camps, see Richard Bernstein, "Experts on Islam Pointing Fingers at One Another," *New York Times* (3 November 2001), sec. A, 13.

In my mind's eye, I try to visualize an encounter between this distinguished crowd and some of their eminent predecessors like Hienrich Heine, Abraham Geiger, Gustav Weil, Franz Rosenthal and the great Ignaz Goldziher. What would these pro-Islamic Jews have to say to their descendants, whose scholarship demeans and denigrates the societies they study? Would Geiger and Goldziher embrace Lewis and Kedourie, or would they be repelled by the latter's new brand of Zionist Orientalism?

CHAPTER FIVE[1]

Is Eurocentrism Unique?

"*And (remember) when his Lord tried Abraham with (His) commands, and he fulfilled them, He said: Lo! I have appointed thee a leader for mankind. (Abraham) said: And of my offspring (will there be leaders)? He said: My covenant includeth not wrong-doers.*"

Qur'ān: 2:124

"*Neither Roman nor Arab, Greek nor Egyptian, Persian nor Mongol ever took himself and his own perfectness with such disconcerting seriousness as the modern white man.*"

W. E. B. Du Bois (1920)[2]

February 4, 2002

I hope to make a modest start in this essay towards a historical and comparative study of autocentrism, defined as the tendency of social groups to claim superior attributes, racial or cultural, and, conversely, to denigrate other groups.

---

[1] This paper first appeared in *Science and Society* 67, 2 (Summer 2003): 205-17. © Science and Society.

[2] W. E. B. Du Bois, "The Souls of White Folk," in: *Darkwater: Voices from Within the Veil* (New York: Harcourt Brace and Howe, 1920), reprinted in: *Monthly Review*, November 2003: 48.

In his essay, *Eurocentrism*, Samir Amin draws a sharp distinction between the "banal provincialism" of medieval Europe and the Eurocentric thought of modern Europe.[3] Amin's distinction hinges on the balance of power between two competing groups. Medieval Europe and Dar-al-Islam were equals, or near equals, in military power, neither able to impose its vision on the other; yet each imagined itself superior to the other. Presumably, such claims of superiority are encountered throughout history; that is what makes them banal. On the other hand, Eurocentrism is not only historically specific to modern, capitalist Europe, it is the product of an asymmetric relationship; it constructs an ideology of racial superiority to support capitalist Europe's project of global domination. Eurocentrism "implies a theory of world history and, departing from it, a global political project."

This approach to Eurocentrism contains important insights, but the sharp distinction it draws between "banal provincialism" and Eurocentrism raises questions. Modern capitalism does not offer the first occasion when one group has gained ascendancy over another; in fact, this has been quite common. Once we broaden our study to take in *all* autocentrisms, between symmetric and asymmetric groups, we need to address a variety of questions. Have stronger groups in asymmetric relationships always mobilized ideologies of differences to perpetuate their superiority? And have they always employed the language of race, blood or lineage? Can there be an autocentrism of weaker groups in asymmetric relationships? Is their autocentrism different from the autocentrism of stronger groups? Should we expect a difference between autocentrisms which justify existing inequalities, projected inequalities or imagined inequalities? Is Eurocentrism different from other autocentrisms that supported the ascendancy of other groups?

---

[3] Samir Amin, *Eurocentrism* (New York: Monthly Review Press, 1989): 74-5.

In order to begin to answer these questions, we need to develop a framework – however elementary, at this stage – that looks at ideologies of group differences, where a group may be defined by its ethnicity, class, lineage, race or gender. As a first step, I proceed to identify the markers that might be employed to define group differences. Next, I examine the sources of autocentrism; in particular, whether asymmetric relationships tend to deepen autocentrism. I then turn to history to examine *how* a variety of groups – the ancient Greeks, Islamicate societies, medieval and modern Europeans, and the Chinese – have articulated their differences from other groups that were equal to, or weaker than, them. Finally, I examine whether our *a priori* expectations explain the historical results.

Group Differences: The Markers

One group of humans may be set apart from others by one or more markers, defined as physical, cultural or social characteristics, which are easily discernible.

The most common physical marker is skin color. Historically, descriptions of skin color have ranged from black, brown and white to yellow, red and blue. In addition to skin color, and often correlated with it, are the color of the hair, ranging from black and brown to red and blonde; the texture of the hair, ranging from straight, wavy, curly to kinky; the shape of the nose, straight, aquiline or flat; or shape of the lips, thin or thick. Finally, there are differences of gender, male and female; and differences of age, children, youth and the old.

The two most common cultural markers are language and religion. In terms of group articulation, it is tempting to divide the world into those who speak ones language and those who do not – this was often the definition of the 'Other.' To the Greeks, the *barbaroi* were all those who did not speak Greek; and to the Arabs, those who did not speak Arabic were *'ajami*, dumb. Differences of religion too have served as important markers, especially when this leads to visible differences in dress, dietary rules, sexual practices, religious architecture and holidays.

The social markers span differences in the ways people make a living or their class affiliations. In terms of the former, groups may be divided into hunters, pastoralists, agriculturalists or city-dwellers. In terms of class relations, people are often divided into binary groups, such as masters and slaves, lords and serfs, or capitalists and workers. It would be easy to think of finer social subdivisions.

These differences may be viewed as variants, part of the diversity of the world of humans and their cultures, without any rank-ordering. Alternatively, a group may rank-order these differences, where their own markers are seen to possess, or become associated with, superior values. A group may trace its own markers backwards to a superior climate or genetic endowment, or attribute it to divine favors. Presumably, this ensures that their superior markers have an enduring basis, and are not rooted in historical accidents.

A group may assign greater aesthetic value to its own markers. The members of a group may define standards of beauty in terms of their own physical or cultural markers, so that all departures from these standards become repulsive. Or they may link their own markers to other desirable attributes, such as greater vigor, creativity, rationality, order, morality or love of freedom. In addition, these superior attributes may be used to explain greater historical achievements, including a more advanced economy, a greater inventiveness, superior political institutions or greater power.

The intensity of a group's *autocentrism* depends on the degree to which it places a greater aesthetic value on its own markers, links them to superior capabilities and historical achievements, and finds the basis of its superiority in climate, divine choices or biology rather than in the processes of history. As autocentrism elevates one group, it may simultaneously downgrade other groups by assigning absolutely lower values to their markers, capabilities and achievements.

Sources of Autocentrism

Although there are many forces, complex, cumulative and subtle, which interact to determine the extent of a group's autocentrism – elevating one's own group and denigrating others – it may be useful to examine how this might be affected by relations of unequal power.

When one group enters into an unequal relationship with another, this creates inducements for the stronger group to construct autocentric ideas. It may be flattering for the stronger group to believe that its dominance is rooted in superior capabilities: that it is *not* accidental – and, therefore, undeserved and temporary. Soon myths will emerge, with or without the encouragement of the state, which endow the stronger group with a history of superior capabilities.

The thesis of unequal capabilities may also serve to rationalize an unequal relationship. It is claimed that the superior capabilities of the stronger group benefit the weaker groups; they help the latter by providing better governance, or teaching them skills and endowing them with institutions which they could not have acquired on their own. This civilizing mission has two advantages. It binds the stronger group to its roles of dominance, and it may reconcile the weaker group to its subjugation.

The stronger group may also be looking for ways to immunize its morally sensitive members against compassion for the weaker group, especially as members of the subject group are used in ways that violate the norms of humane behavior. This may be done in two ways. It may be shown that the weaker group is sub-human, culturally or biologically. The weaker group engages in behavior that is contemptible, because it violates the norms of the stronger group. Alternatively, they may be excluded from the human species, thereby excluding them from human sympathies.

In the long run, the autocentric myths are not likely to survive if they lack a modicum of plausibility. The greater the advantage actually enjoyed by the stronger group – in living standards, technology and power – the greater the credibility of these myths; they appear to explain the visible signs of superiority of the stronger group. Conversely, when the weaker group lags visibly, it makes sense to attribute their lag to their inferior capabilities. It follows that if the lags increase over time, this may reinforce the autocentric myths.

In an unequal relationship, the stronger group is likely to dominate and, in some cases, monopolize the production of knowledge. The weaker group may be unable to rectify or oppose the 'knowledge' about them produced by the stronger group. *A fortiori*, they may also lack the means to oppose the autocentric myths of the strong with their own; these myths may, however, be opposed by dissenters within the stronger group. Most likely, this asymmetry has increased in modern times, when weaker groups are more easily excluded from the institutions – universities, publishing houses, and mass media – which produce social knowledge. In earlier periods, weaker groups could create their own social knowledge through epics, ballads and folktales.

Ideologies are not constructed *de novo*. They are likely to draw upon historical narratives, coded in religious cannons, myths, memories and patterns from the past. Where these narratives glorify a particular group or denigrate others, they can be mobilized to justify and deepen present inequalities. On the other hand, if the sacred cannons reject racist ideas, they will oppose the new-fangled myths of inequalities, diluting their impact and perhaps neutralize them over time.

It should not be supposed, however, that autocentrisms cannot emerge between groups that are equal or nearly equal; though, they are likely to lose some of their force under these conditions. When two equal groups are in competition – and their competition gets intense or is seen to be a zero-sum game – both may engage in autocentrism. Each side may mobilize autocentric myths to reinforce unity in its own ranks, to fire the cupidity and ambition of its own members, or to win allies amongst kindred groups by playing upon their fear of rival groups.

The limits to such autocentrism should also be obvious. Since the two groups are equal or nearly equal, their autocentric constructs cannot deviate too far from the facts, or they risk losing credibility. Unless they are insulated from each other, the autocentric constructs of each group are also open to challenge from the other group; this too will restrain the autocentric constructs. Further, it would be unwise for any group facing a formidable antagonist to seriously underestimate its capabilities; it may represent its rivals as cruel but it would be unwise to paint them as stupid. There is another risk to carrying the autocentric myths too far. Once you have painted your rivals as inhuman monsters, it becomes hard to engage in negotiations with them when the competition becomes too costly. This too may restrain the intensity of the autocentric narrative.

A Variety of Autocentrisms

As I review a variety of autocentrisms across space and time, there is no pretense that the assessments offered are definitive or always rooted in exhaustive evidence.

Determining the extent of autocentrism in any group can be problematic. A group's autocentrism may change over time, and it may vary across different classes at any point in time. Moreover, too often we rely on literary sources – the writings of philosophers, historians, poets and playwrights – as our primary sources for evaluating autocentrism. This has pitfalls. These literary sources may reflect an elitist viewpoint; they may be harbingers of things to come; or they may never gain wider acceptance. In the event, we need to look out for discriminatory practices, whether sanctioned by laws or custom, that may be rooted in autocentric ideologies. I take these to be more reliable indicators of autocentrism.

Ancient Greece. It appears that the Greeks first acquired a consciousness of their distinctiveness – Hellenic, Greek-speaking, separate from the barbarians – in the eighth century BCE. However, this was not accompanied by a sense of superiority, which emerged much later, during the fifth and fourth centuries BCE, in the course of their rivalry with the Persians.[4]

The sense of Greek superiority finds its most rigorous expression in Aristotle's *Politics*. He argues that barbarians are deficient in reasoning and lack the ability to govern – and hence, they are "by nature" fit to be slaves, whereas the Greeks are born to be free and to govern others.[5] Aristotle's autocentrism finds the clearest expression in his claim that the Hellenes occupy an intermediate position between the Europeans and the Asiatics. The Europeans are free-spirited but lack intelligence, while the Asiatics possess intelligence and skills but lack freedom. The Greeks combine the virtues of both, while avoiding their defects. That is why they remain "free and best

---

[4] Shlaifer (1936: 166-7) and Reger (2000: 105) argue that the autocentrism of this period – the equation of Persians with barbarians – was a nationalistic response to the Persian wars. Robert Shlaifer, "Greek Theories of Slavery from Homer to Aristotle," *Harvard Studies in Classical Philology* 47 (1936): 165-204. Gary Reger, "Enslavement and manumission in ancient Greece," in: Berel Lang, ed., *Race and Racism in Theory and Practice* (Lanham, MA.: Rowman and Littlefield, 2000).

[5] Peter L. Phillips Simpson, *The Politics of Aristotle* (Chapel Hill: University of North Carolina Press, 1997): 9-10.

governed," and, if they were united, they would be capable of "ruling everyone.''[6]

It appears, however, that Aristotle represented a minority position. He acknowledges that "others" maintain that "it is by law that one person is a slave and another a master, whereas by nature there is no difference at all."[7] Even Aristotle's arguments should not be equated with modern racism; the barbarians he excluded are not a racial category.[8] Most remarkably, when Alexander conquered the Asiatics, he ignored the counsel of Aristotle, his teacher. He refused to treat the defeated Persians as "natural slaves." Instead, his policies show that he wanted to create a joint Macedonian-Persian world empire.[9]

Medieval Islamdom. There are two organizing principles that medieval Islamdom employed in classifying societies: one based on faith, another on climatic zones.

Islamicate society was a community of faith, whose membership depended only on the acceptance of Islam, not on color, class, lineage or ethnicity. In theory, at least during the early period of Islamdom, this community of faith, *Dar al-Islam* (the House of Peace), was set apart from *Dar al-Harb* (the House of War). Islamicate rulers were required to wage constant war against *Dar al-Harb*, though periods of respite were permitted. The wars could cease only

---

[6] Simpson (1997): 127.

[7] Simpson, 1997: 13. According to Shlaifer (1997: 168-9), "By the time of Aristotle, there had arisen a large body of opinion, which maintained that popular prejudice against the barbarian was entirely unjustified."

[8] Snowden (1995: 23) reflects the opinion of most scholars when he writes that while the Greeks and Romans commented on the "obviously different physical characteristics of Ethiopians" they did not develop "an elaborate and rigid system of discrimination based on color of the skin." Similarly, Reger (2000: 99) writes that "Ancient slavery was color-blind." Frank M. Snowden, "Europe's Oldest Chapter in the History of Black-White Relations," in: Benjamin P. Bowser, ed., *Racism and Anti-Racism in World Perspective* (Thousand Oaks, CA.: Sage Publications, 1995).

[9] Reger (2000): 105.

when the *Dar al-Harb* was incorporated into *Dar al-Islam*.[10]

Once the non-Muslims entered into *Dar al-Islam* they were granted rights as *dhimmis* or protected subjects. They did not serve in the military, and enjoyed varying degrees of autonomy over their civil affairs. On the other hand, they paid the *jizya*, a poll tax, but this did not apply to slaves, old or sick men, women, children and monks. At times, Islamic law also subjected non-Muslims to a variety of humiliating social restrictions, though these were not always enforced. At first, the *dhimmi* status was accorded only to Christians and Jews, but over time it was extended to nearly all non-Muslim groups.[11]

In their climatic ethnology, Islamdom clearly followed Greek and Roman precedents. They divided the northern hemisphere – the inhabitable world – into seven latitudinal zones. It is the central zones – the third and fourth zones, neither too hot nor too cold – that possessed the greatest potential for supporting civilized societies. These zones contained the central Arab lands, North Africa, Iran, the northern Mediterranean and parts of China. The first and second zones, because of their extreme heat, and the sixth and seventh zones, because of their extreme cold, did not support advanced civilizations.[12] This climatic principle was not applied too rigidly. Although much of India and Arabia fell within the first and second zones, both were peninsulas, which allowed for cooling and brought them closer to the temperate climate of the central zones. This explains the high level of civilization attained by these two regions.[13]

---

[10] Ann Lambton, *State and Government in Medieval Islam* (New York: Oxford University Press, 1981): 13, 201-5.

[11] Lambton, 1981: 203-7.

[12] Aziz Al-Azmeh, "Barbarians in Arab eyes," *Past and Present* 134 (February 1992): 3-18; and Carole Hillenbrand, *The Crusades: Islamic Perspective* (NY: Routledge, 2000): 268-74.

[13] Al-Azmeh (1992): 8.

It should be noted that the essential thrust of this climatic ethnology – that civilizational achievements were correlated with climatic zones – had some basis in facts at the time. Nearly every one of the advanced civilizations and the great empires, both ancient and medieval, were located in the central zones. On the other hand, the achievements of the peoples inhabiting the cold and hot zones – the Slavs, Turks, Bulgars, Franks, Sudanese and Ethiopians – were not comparable to those of the central zones.

There are other reasons for thinking that ideology may not have been the principal motivation behind this climatic construct. First, the cold and hot zones were far removed from the Islamicate heartlands, allowing a freer play to the imagination in the description of these remote regions. Second, the denigration of peoples in the north and south was never complete. Thus, while the Franks are seen as coarse, filthy, sexually lax, and lacking in the sciences, they are also described as courageous, enterprising, disciplined and well-governed.[14] Third, these regions did not constitute serious threats to the Islamic empire, at least during the early phase of Islamicate conquests, when these constructs were developed. Finally, the central zones were not wholly Arab or Islamic; they included, both in medieval and ancient times, a variety of non-Islamic communities. The Muslim sources were nearly always very generous in recognizing the achievements of Egyptian, Greek, Babylonian, Indian and Chinese civilizations.[15]

The West, Medieval and Early Modern. In defining their self-image, the West – collectively or its several components – has not

---

[14] Hillenbrand, 2000: 270-74.

[15] See Al-Andalusi's (11th century/1991) description of scientifically productive nations, including Indians, Persians, Chaldeans, Greeks, Romans, Egyptians and Israelites. Said Al-Andalusi, *Science in the medieval world*, translators, Sema'an I. Salem and Alok Kumar (Austin: University of Texas Press, 1991).

only drawn upon differences in religion, culture and climate, but from an early date we encounter claims to superiority rooted in biological metaphors – blood, stock, color, lineage and race – which gained greater salience over time. We also observe a tendency, again quite early on, to translate the ideologies of differences into systems of legal discrimination and worse.

Although Christianity was initially a Mediterranean religion – spanning three continents – it would acquire a European identity starting in the seventh century. This was the result of two parallel processes. While they destroyed the Roman Empire, the Germanic invaders soon embraced Latin Christianity and carried it – through wars, colonization and missionary work – to the northern regions of Europe. This replaced the political unity of the defunct Roman Empire with a deeper cultural unity based in Christianity, a common language (Latin), and a hierarchy of priests centered in Rome. At the same time, as the Islamicate Empire incorporated Christian domains in the Levant, North Africa, Spain and much of the Mediterranean, a politically fragmented Europe increasingly emphasized its Christian identity. This identity found early expression in the wars against heretics, persecution of Jews, and the demonization of Islam.[16]

The three remaining components of Western autocentrism – a superior geography, race and divine preferment – were derived from ancient Greece and Israel. Although the Greeks had two systems of ordering the world – the division into three continents and the division into seven latitudinal climes – it is perhaps not too difficult to

---

[16] In 1215, the Fourth Lateran Council threatened to excommunicate Christian rulers who refused to exterminate heretics (Muldoon, 2000: 84). On medieval Europe's demonization of Islam, see Southern (1962). James Muldoon, "Race or Culture: Medieval Notions of Difference," in: Berel Lang, ed., *Race and Racism in Theory and Practice* (Lanham, MA.: Rowman and Littlefield, 2000). R. W. Southern, *Western Views of Islam in the Middle Ages* (Cambridge: Harvard University Press, 1962).

understand why medieval Europe opted for the former. The climatic scheme placed northern Europe in the less desirable fifth and sixth zones, whose cold and frigid temperatures, so the Greeks argued, did not support intellectual vigor or high civilization. On the other hand, the continental system allowed Europeans to appropriate one of three equal continents and endow it with a temperate climate.

The continental system had another advantage in constructing a European autocentrism: it allocated one continent to each of the three sons of Noah. Hay has shown that a racial and continental construction of the Noachian legend began with Josephus, a Jewish scholar of the first century BCE, and was firmly established by fifth century ACE.[17] The biblical prophecy, which granted the progeny of Japheth dominion over the children of Shem and Ham, was converted into an ideology of racial domination by identifying Japheth with Europe, Shem with Asia, and Ham with Africa. By the same prophecy, the Hamites, identified with Africans, would serve both Europe and Asia.

There is some disagreement about whether ethnicity in early medieval Europe was a social or racial construct. It is clear that the discourse about ethnicity, even in this early period, was framed in terms of racial concepts, including blood, stock, gens and natio; but Bartlett believes that "its medieval reality was almost entirely cultural."[18] In disagreeing, Hoffman maintains that the use of such terms by medieval writers shows "a fundamentally biological explanation of how the groups came into being."[19] In any case, even Bartlett

---

[17] Denys Hay, *Europe: The Emergence of an Idea* (Edinburgh: University Press, 1957): 1-15.

[18] Robert Bartlett, *The Making of Europe* (Princeton, NJ.: Princeton University Press, 1993): 197.

[19] Richard Hoffman, "Outsiders by Birth and Blood: Racist Ideology and Realities Around the Periphery of Medieval European Culture," *Studies in Medieval and Renaissance History* 6 (1983): 3.

speaks of an "intensification of racial feeling in the later Middle Ages" that was accompanied by a "new biological racism."[20]

The later Middle Ages are also marked by legal discrimination against native populations in Europe's periphery: including Ireland, Wales and the Slavic areas conquered, colonized or recently converted to Christianity by the Germans and Franks. Starting in the fourteenth century, the towns and guilds in these areas began to restrict membership by race; residential areas were segregated by race; languages and cultural practices belonging to native populations were banned; and marriage between conquering and native populations was prohibited.[21] According to Bartlett, "Ghettoization and discrimination marked the later centuries of the Middle Ages."[22]

The class conflict, between lords and serfs, during the Middle Ages is also framed in the language of racism, lineage in this case. The medieval writers – including the church fathers, nobles and artists – commonly describe the serfs as stupid, malformed, grotesque, dwelling in filth and excrement, and closer to beasts than humans. In addition, this degradation of serfs is attributed to their lineage, their connection to the accursed line of Cain, Ham or both. In short, the serfs are savages who are fitted by nature, or their inherited sins, to the hard and humiliating conditions to which they are born.[23]

The idiom of race enters into Europe's autocentric discourse in a variety of contexts during the early modern period. While the persecution, expulsion and forced conversion of Jews and Muslims in

---

[20] Bartlett (1993): 237.

[21] Bartlett (1993): chapters 8 and 9; Nicholas P. Canny, "The Ideology of English Colonization: From Ireland to America," in: David Armitage, ed., Theories of Empire, 1450-1800 (Aldershot: Ashgate, 1998).

[22] Bartlett (1993): 239.

[23] Paul Freedman, *Images of the Medieval Peasant* (Stanford: Stanford University Press, 1999): chs. 4 and 6.

Spain may have been motivated primarily by Christian bigotry, conversion did not win the Conversos and Moriscos, as the converted Jews and Muslims were called, acceptance into Spanish society. Careers in the church and state were restricted to those who could prove a Christian lineage before the Inquisition; and the Moriscos were eventually expelled in the early seventeenth century. Lewis concludes that what had begun as a "general religious prejudice soon became primarily one about lineage, and blood became a pronounced idiom of socioracial difference."[24]

In the Americas, the Spaniards quickly constructed a system of racial discrimination to justify their exploitation of the indigenous Indians. According to Liss, they lost no time in imposing a "rudimentary apartheid policy" under which a white Spanish elite extracted labor and goods from the dark Indians.[25] In 1550, Juan Sepúlveda, the royal chaplain and philosopher, produced an elaborate defense of these policies. He argued that the Indians practiced cannibalism, offered human sacrifices, and were sexual deviants; in other words, they were less than human. Drawing upon Aristotle, he maintained that the Indians were deficient in reason. They were like children compared to adults and, hence, they were naturally fitted to be slaves.[26]

Although some medieval writers identified Africans as descendents of Ham, according to Drake, their systematic denigration as an inferior, savage race began only after the mid-fifteenth century when their blackness became a "master symbol" of all negative racial

---

[24] Laura A. Lewis, "Spanish Ideology and the Practice of Inequality in the New World," in: Benjamin P. Bowser, ed., *Racism and Anti-Racism in World Perspective* (Thousand Oaks, CA.: Sage Publications, 1995): 48.

[25] Peggy K. Liss, *Mexico under Spain, 1521-1556: Society and the Origins of Nationality* (Chicago: University of Chicago Press, 1975): 43.

[26] Lewis, 1995: 50-2.

characteristics.[27] In Spanish Americas, the ban on enslavement of Indians, introduced in 1542, would not be extended to Africans. Vaughan and Vaughan attest to the "sheer accumulation of derogatory references [to blacks] in narratives, plays, poems, and other printed and visual material in the second half of the sixteenth century" in Elizabethan England, and these denigrative images "transcended class, gender, age and levels of literacy."[28] During the last years of her reign, Queen Elizabeth was already calling "repeatedly, though unsuccessfully, for the expulsion from her realm of "negars" and "Blackamoorers." A hundred years later, according to Wood, the English colonists in North America, "who had traditionally identified themselves as Christians began for the first time to distinguish themselves as Whites."[29]

China. The Chinese have always cultivated a sense of superiority; they inhabited the Central Kingdom, surrounded on all sides by barbarians. However, this superiority was based on cultural rather than biological distinctions, barring one aberrant flirtation with racism starting in late nineteenth century.[30] This cultural ordering, with China at the center, was already central to the Zhou order (1122 to 256 BCE) which distinguished between "states whose rulers belonged to the Zhou political and cultural order, and others who did not." The Chinese texts rarely contain any references to

---

[27] St. Clair Drake, *Black Folk Here and There* (2 vols.) (Los Angeles: University of California Center for Afro-American Studies, 1990): 2, 192

[28] Alden T. Vaughan and Virginia Mason Vaughan, "Before *Othello*: Elizabethan Representations of Sub-Saharan Africans," *The William and Mary Quarterly* 54, 1 (January 1997): 42,43.

[29] Peter H. Wood, "If Toads Could Speak": How the myth of Race Took Hold and Flourished in the Minds of Europe's Renaissance Colonizers," in: Benjamin P. Bowser, ed., *Racism and Anti-Racism in World Perspective* (Thousand Oaks, CA.: Sage Publications, 1995): 37.

[30] W. J. F. Jenner, "Race and History in China," *New Left Review* 11 (September-October 2001): 58; Kung-chuan Hsiao, *A History of Chinese Political Thought*, volume one, tr. F. W. Mote (Princeton: Princeton University Press, 1979): 137.

the physical appearance of barbarians. It is striking that a biological racism did not enter into the Chinese discourse even during the three centuries of "endemic ethnic conflict" that began in the late third century CE.[31]

The centrality of culture – rather than race – in the Chinese worldview had an important corollary. Nearly always, this translated into a civilizing mission rooted in the premise that "the barbarians could be culturally assimilated; *laihua*, 'come and be transformed,' or *hanhua*, 'become Chinese.'[32] In the Confucian cannon, the chief instrument of this civilizing mission was always education. This policy produced not only an expansion of the boundaries of the Chinese state but the eventual absorption of the conquered peoples into the Chinese cultural sphere.

The exception to this occurs towards the end of the nineteenth century. Once China's self-image as the Central Kingdom had been dismantled by the Opium wars, China's reformers adapted to the reality of Western dominance by giving a racial content to their sense of superiority. They sought to reconstitute Chinese nationalism on a racial basis; the Han Chinese were seen as one big family descended from the Yellow Emperor. Unable to support their cultural superiority, they imitated the racist ideology of the West, inserting the Han Chinese nearly at the top, just below the dominant Whites. Sun Yatsen, the leader of the Chinese nationalist movement, spoke of Chineseness "running in the blood." In time, this became a central part of the ideology of the Guomindang dictatorship in Taiwan.

---

[31] Jenner (2001): 58, 61.

[32] Frank Dikötter, "Group Definition and the Idea of 'Race' in Modern China (1793-1949)," *Ethnic and Racial Studies* 13, 3 (July 1990): 421.

Concluding Remarks

The review of autocentrism across four civilizations – Greek, Islamdom, European and Sinic – has yielded results which are more often at variance with *a priori* expectations.

Our theoretical analysis suggested that stronger groups in asymmetric relationships are likely to adopt autocentric constructs towards weaker groups. In two of the four cases surveyed in this paper, this was not generally true. The ancient Greeks adopted an attitude of superiority towards the Asiatics only briefly, during the fourth century BCE, when the Persians threatened them with wars. In fact, the most active centers of Hellenic civilization moved east after Alexander's conquest, and it was there, in partnership with the Asiatics that it continued to flourish for several more centuries. Similarly, the power of Islamicate societies was rarely founded, in theory or practice, on a racial stratification. The Islamicate elites claimed cultural superiority not for particular races, but for peoples living in central climatic zones, which included several peoples other than themselves.

In a third case, where the Chinese were for more than three thousand years the dominant party in contacts with a variety of non-Chinese ethnic groups, their autocentric constructs did not generally employ the language of race or lineage. While the Chinese empires claimed centrality, this was based on cultural distinctions between themselves and the weaker groups. More importantly, the Chinese fully assimilated nearly all the barbarians they subjugated.

It would appear that the Europeans – or the West, more generally – are the exceptions to this. The evidence suggests that stronger groups in Europe, starting as early as the twelfth century, rather quickly moved towards the language of superiority, denigrating the weaker groups as culturally and, just as often, racially inferior. This may be observed in their relations with subjugated populations – the Irish, Slavs, Conversos, Moriscos, American Indians and Africans – both inside and outside Europe. More to the point, the autocentric myths were translated into discriminatory policies – sometimes, genocidal policies – against the weaker groups.

This means that Samir Amin's construction of Eurocentrism as a capitalist ideology, though fundamentally correct, needs to be modified in one important respect. It appears that the racist conceptions that underpin this ideology are not unique to the capitalist epoch; they represent habits of thought going back to medieval Europe. The Franks, Germans, English and Spaniards used race to justify their dominance over subject populations well before global capitalism and global inequalities had been firmly established. The roots of European racism are older than capitalism.

What then are the sources of European racism – the recurrent tendency of dominant European groups, both medieval and modern, to employ metaphors of race, blood, pedigree and lineage in defining their autocentric constructs? It would be futile to speculate without further enquiry whether the sources of this propensity lie in the material conditions of life – some aspect of feudal organization, or perhaps a more intense struggle for survival amongst ethnic groups in Western Europe which required stronger group solidarity – the excessive concern with genealogy and the ranking of families, tribes and ethnicities in biblical narratives; or some legacy of Germanic tribal past, which may perhaps be yet preserved in Germanic languages. This question can only be explored in another essay.

PART TWO

Arabs and the United States

CHAPTER SIX

A History of September 11

"Lo! The noblest of you in the sight of Allah, is the best in conduct."

Qur'ān: 49:13

November 8, 2001[1]

Occasionally, a student at Northeastern University, troubled by my analysis of US foreign policy, will challenge me with the question, 'Why are you here if you don't like the United States?'

I answer that this is the most rational thing to do. I came to the United States only after I had tried living in several countries on four different continents. I was born in Palestine, but the Zionists took over that country in 1948, and the Haganah expelled my family from our ancestral village in Galilee. We moved to Korea, but the Americans soon followed us there with a devastating war to defend their 'freedom.' My next destination was democratic Iran, but a CIA-inspired military coup overthrew its government in 1953. I left the medieval city of Isfahan when the coup plotters restored the Shah to the Peacock Throne. One after another, I tried living in Congo, Chile,

[1] This essay started as a talk delivered at a symposium on September 11 at Northeastern University.

Nicaragua and Guatemala, but each time the CIA destabilized these countries. In 1988, after many misadventures, I finally understood that there is only one country the CIA would never destabilize: the United States. That is when I moved to Massachusetts.

I wish to present for your consideration two verses from the Qur'ān; they will explain my *locus standi* as a social scientist. (I am assuming that this is still permissible; the President has told us repeatedly that the US is not at war against Islam, only against Islamic terrorists.)

> *O Mankind! Be careful of your duty to your Lord Who created you from a single soul and from it created its mate and from them twain spread abroad a multitude of men and women.* (4:1)

> *O mankind! Lo! We have created you male and female, and have made you nations and tribes that you may know one another.* (49:13)

Mark the words. God speaks to humankind: not to the Israelites, not to the Arabs, not to whites or blacks, but to all of humanity. Mark the words. God speaks to men *and* women. Mark the words. God reminds us that we carry the same genes *because* we have the same parents. Mark again the words. God says: Your differences are a blessing: they provide you with opportunities for getting to know each other, to learn from each other, and to compete with each other in doing good works.

Twelve hundred years later, we come across a human document, *The Declaration of Independence*, which proclaims the "self-evident" truth that "all Men are created equal, that they are endowed by their Creator with certain inalienable Rights, that among these are Life, Liberty and the Pursuit of Happiness." It is time to ask again, before the anger of September 11 consumes us, if we have upheld this "self-evident truth" in this great country, especially in our dealings with Africa, Latin America and Asia.

I will avoid the temptation to explore the meaning of September 11 in the language of tribalism, in terms of *them* and *us*. In these critical times, we should try harder than ever not to privilege any country, race or people. It is also vital that we locate these attacks in time, in the matrix of historical time, and not view them through the prism of selected images that are being played up *ad nauseum* on our television screens. Only by acquiring a historical understanding of September 11, we can hope to avoid the silly line of thinking that says, "We were attacked because *we* are so good; and they hate us because *they* are so evil."

Our world was created in two great waves of European expansion that eventually created a global capitalist system. The first wave, starting in 1492, broke against the shores of the Americas, and very quickly led to the extermination of much of its Amerindian population. It also impacted the Africans, who were imported into the Americas as slaves to replace the dead Indians. Starting around 1800, the Industrial Revolution spurred the second wave of expansion, which was directed against all peoples of color and, before the end of the nineteenth century, it had led to the colonization of nearly all of Africa and Asia. Core capital penetrated these two continents and restructured or degraded their economies to produce cheap primary goods for export to the Core countries.

This global capitalist system follows a powerful logic. It creates deepening economic, social and military inequalities between rich and poor societies. The Core capitalists, based in the most advanced capitalist countries, use their economic power and military might to create and dominate world markets; they control or colonize the weaker states. This ensures that capital, technology and skills accumulate in the Core countries, while the Periphery provides mostly cheap labor and cheap resources.

This global system of inequalities is not stable. Marx thought that it is unstable because of a class contradiction at the heart of capitalism, between the capitalists – the propertied classes – and the dispossessed workers. He believed that the workers in the Core countries are a revolutionary force: they would eventually overthrow the system, expropriate the capitalists, and create a socialist society. This did not happen.

However, the global system produced two additional contradictions that were more potent. The Core countries and would-be Core countries competed to acquire *exclusive* control over markets and resources in the Periphery. In addition, the expropriated classes in the Periphery were gradually mobilizing, under nationalist and socialist ideologies, to end foreign control over their lives. These contradictions precipitated two 'World Wars' – in the first half of the twentieth century – between two sets of countries at the Core. In turn, the first War precipitated the Russian Revolution, and both, cumulatively, advanced the dismantling of colonial empires starting in the late 1940s.

This was a historical window of opportunity, but it did not bring relief to all countries at the Periphery. China and India, for different reasons, were among the leading beneficiaries; they emerged as unified countries under strong liberation movements committed to sovereignty and development. The Arabs and Africans were not so lucky. Their lands had been vivisected by the imperialist powers; they gained independence as fragmented entities, still dominated by Britain, France and, increasingly, the United States. In addition, the great powers inserted a new contradiction – Israel, a Jewish colonial-settler state – in the heart of the Islamicate world.

This window of opportunity could not last forever: it began to close starting in the 1980s. In 1990, with the collapse of the Soviet Union, the counterpoise to the United States was gone. Having learned to manage their rivalries during the Cold War, the Core countries had become partners in imperialism, with the United States in the lead. This partnership produced a dramatic result: it restored the old imperialism in new forms.

The World Bank, IMF and the newly created WTO quickly assumed the functions of a quasi-world government – an international bureaucracy backed by the Core countries – defining and policing the new global economic regime. Increasingly, after 1990, this global triad opened up the markets of the former East Bloc and Third World countries for domination by multinational corporations from the Core countries.

These changes greatly diminished the standing of the Periphery in the global system. The Core countries now worked in tandem as never before; also, they commanded greater military and economic superiority – vis-à-vis the Periphery – than they did at the previous height of their power in the 1890s. The ruling classes in much of the Periphery have been completely co-opted; and, in Latin America and the Arab/Islamicate countries, they wage open warfare against their own peoples. These contradictions are deepest in the Arab world, which labors under a four-fold burden. It is subjugated because it is a part of the Periphery; it is subjugated for its oil; it is subjugated in order to facilitate Israeli expansionism; and it is subjugated because of lingering historical animosities. Of course, Western triumphalists declared that this was a perfect world. Their leading representative, Francis Fukuyama, concluded that history had ended: it had arrived at its final destination. The West had finally created a world that "is completely satisfying to human beings in their most essential characteristics."

The attacks of September 11 are a reminder that history has no terminus. Far from having ended in the 1990s, the contradictions of history have deepened, forcing long-simmering conflicts to the surface. The tectonic plates of the global system are rubbing harder against each other. We are witnessing the first eruptions of conflicts – between the Core and the Periphery and within these two segments of the global economy – that have so far been papered over by a media and academia servile to the interests of corporate capital. Once again, we live in a world whose rules have been restructured to the advantage of the richest, both globally and within each country. Globalization and global poverty do not mix well. A growing cabal of billionaires, more visible and more united that before, now confronts growing masses of starving, desperate and angry people in every quadrant of the globe.

In concluding, I wish to invite all Americans – with one of the highest proportions of college graduates anywhere in the world – to reflect on the conditions that forced them, more than two hundred years ago, to rebel against the legal and established authority of Britain, the 'mother country' of the American colonies. This is how *The Declaration of Independence* justified this rebellion:

> "… when a long Train of Abuses and Usurpation, pursuing invariably the same Object, evinces a Design to reduce them under absolute Despotism, it is their Right, it is their Duty, to throw off such Government, and to provide new Guards for their future Security. Such has been the patient Sufferance of these Colonies; and such is now the Necessity which constrains them to alter their former Systems of Government."

In all fairness, can the honorable citizens of the United States, 'the greatest country in the world,' deny the oppressed peoples of the world today the same Right, the same Duty, to follow the same line of Reasoning, and carry it to the same Conclusion – restore their Inalienable Rights? Can we grant that the Wretched of the Earth have a Right, as Americans did, to seize their own Freedom?

CHAPTER SEVEN

Race and Visibility

"Surely We created man of the best stature. Then We reduced him to the lowest of the low, save those who believe and do good works, and theirs is a reward unfailing."

Qur'an: 95: 4-6

"Verily, We have honored the children of Adam. We carry them on the land and the sea, and have made provision of good things for them, and have preferred them above many of those whom We created with a marked preferment."

Qur'an: 17:70

December 11, 2001

When I crossed the border into the United States in 1988, after living in Canada for two years, I had the curious feeling that my wife, my son and I, still brown-skinned and dark-haired, had somehow become invisible.

We walked the streets of Hamilton – a small university town in Central New York – or nearby Utica and Syracuse, each of them overwhelmingly white, without attracting any unwanted attention.

The motorists did not gawk at us while we waited at the curb for the walk signal. At restaurants, there were no heads turning in our direction. The shoppers and cashiers did not greet our entry into the stores with a quizzical, perplexed look, following our very steps. Even our neighbors left us alone.

I was relieved at this loss of visibility. It was a signal change from my experience in Canada recently as a professor, and several years before when I was attending graduate school in London, Ontario. The only time I felt comfortable stepping outside the campus was in the cold winter months, when bundled in jacket, hood, scarf and gloves, I became nearly indistinguishable from every one else. In summer, when I had to shed these sartorial covers, I ventured out only at night, under the cover of darkness. I had no wish to invite racial slurs from teenagers, sober or drunk, driving by in their convertibles, pickups and jeeps.

I enjoyed this invisibility even at my teaching job at Northeastern University. Yes, there was a little edginess when I first entered a class, a mild dismay, anticipating the strange accents and manners of 'another Indian professor.' For the most part, I managed to lay these fears to rest, and week after week, my students would concentrate on *what* I had to say, undistracted by *who* said it. However, this invisibility proved to be fragile.

When I began to depart from the scripted texts, drawing attention to the ideological intent of economics, its Eurocentric biases, and its disregard for facts, not a few of my students began to take a harder look at *me*. Over time, as I elaborated my critique, it made me more visible. My ethnicity and origins, my brown skin and dark hair, their texture and opaqueness, began to obstruct their view. I became proof of the absurdity of my critique. I felt like the black carpenter whose comments on the uxorial problems of white clergy invited a sharp rebuke from the philosophic Kant. He declared, "This fellow was quite black from head to foot ... a clear proof that he was stupid."[1]

Then, all of a sudden, September 11 introduced a new dynamic. The nineteen hijackers of Arab and Muslim background, their planes crashing into the Twin Towers, had unleashed a fury that would overthrow many governments, abridge many liberties, and rearrange many lives, here at home and abroad. This first massive attack on Americans on their own soil had shaken America. They were now united – in grief, anger and indignation – against *anyone* ethnically connected to the perpetrators of this undeserved and 'unprovoked' act of violence. Almost instantly, I could sense from my little corner of the world, that this anger, volcanic and intense, would reorder the world in a hurry. Soon, this foreboding came true.

Almost as soon as I walked into the Attleboro station to catch the 6:30 AM train, I noticed a change. One by one, the heads, the eyes, the glances turned to me, as they would towards a suspect, towards a face one recognizes from a poster for the most wanted. The commuters, many of whom had taken this train with me for years, now felt uncomfortable at my presence. In their newborn sense of insecurity, they began to perceive a connection between the hijackers and me. My Pakistani ethnicity was indistinguishable from the Arab background of the nineteen hijackers. A crust of visibility began to thicken around me. I was back in Canada.

The trajectory of America's reaction to September 11 has been unfortunate but predictable. The US administration quickly painted the world in two unmistakable colors, white and black; no shades of gray to confuse the already shaken citizenry. President George Bush had enunciated a new doctrine. "You are either with *us* or you are against us." Ergo, if you are not with us, you are black – and

---

[1] Emmanuel Eze, *Race and Enlightenment: A Reader* (Blackwell: 2000): 38.

that makes for great visibility. This would be a global war, a Manichaean contest, between the United States, symbolizing "infinite justice" and "enduring freedom," and Osama bin Laden, with his global terrorist network, commanding the evil hordes of Islamic totalitarianism.

Instantly, the United States gave Pakistan "a second chance" to prove itself. Without losing a moment, Pakistan's military junta took up the challenge. The attack on Afghanistan was soon unfurled; the mightiest concentration of military power in human history was deployed against a war-ravaged, famine-stricken country. The smart bombs, the cluster bombs, the daisy-cutters, the bunker-busters began to descend on Afghanistan. Not a few fell on villages, hospitals, mosques and Red Cross warehouses.

The Americans opened two additional fronts. The Al-Qaida network would have to be starved of funds. They issued two lists of political parties, financial institutions, charities and individuals suspected of links to Al-Qaida, their assets frozen. More ominously, America began a descent into a Hobbesian state, where the liberties of *some* Americans and *all* aliens would be traded against the security of *other* Americans, 'real' Americans.

The attacks of September 11 led to an instant boom in racially motivated attacks against persons of Arab, Pakistani and other Islamicate ethnicities. This has produced a growing number of arrests and detentions; but when their numbers crossed 1000, the count became a state secret, unavailable to the public. The United States passed new laws and edicts allowing the FBI to tap phones and to enter into homes without notice. The government could now hold aliens, both legal and illegal, without trial for as long as a year. Military courts could try terrorist suspects in secrecy and hang them in the absence of a unanimous verdict.

I am thankful in these dangerous times to be on sabbatical, away from my students, who would be spared, at least for a while, all my talk about the toy economies that falsify reality, abstract from history, and elevate the interests of particular classes and particular nations (USA, among others) to the category of the Universal Good. My sabbatical had freed me at the right time from the unpleasant task of curtailing my own speech. Cloistered in my academic cell, I could become invisible.

I did, however, in the first weeks after September 11, put up a red, white and blue flag on my office door. The inspiration for this came from my wife when she began plastering our front door, mailbox and her car with small paper flags. When a colleague commended me for my patriotism, I answered that I was only exercising my right of free speech – or what was left of it. It was a comic gesture, an ironic attempt to regain the invisibility that I had lost in the aftermath of September 11.

CHAPTER EIGHT

A Clash or Blowback?

"*And if Allah had not repelled some men by others the earth would have been corrupted.*"

Qur'ān: 2:251

"*For had it not been for Allah's repelling some men by means of others, cloisters and churches and oratories and mosques, wherein the name of Allah is oft mentioned, would assuredly have been pulled down.*"

Qur'ān: 22: 40

December 17, 2001

In the weeks after the September 11 attacks, and the instant US declaration of a global war against countries that harbor 'terrorists' – a list populated by Muslim countries – it appeared that the 'clash of civilizations' predicted by Samuel Huntington was underway or just around the corner.[1]

The war rhetoric was deafening, aimed at resurrecting atavistic passions. Instantly, President Bush began casting the attacks in a

[1] Samuel Huntington, "The Clash of Civilizations?" *Foreign Affairs* (Summer 1993): 22-49; and *The Clash of Civilizations and the Remaking of World Order* (New York: Simon and Schuster, 1998).

Manichaean mould. Osama bin Laden and his evil cohorts had declared war against 'all civilized countries' – long a code for the West – and *they* would get the 'Crusade' that they wanted. Osama bin Laden saw the world with equal clarity, divided into two warring camps of believers and infidels. The millennial war between the West and Islamdom was about to be joined. Or, so it seemed.

September 11 will remain a day inscribed in infamy. But does it mark the first strike in a clash of civilizations predicted by our sage political scientist? Samuel Huntington prevaricates, but he sticks to his guns. In an interview, he declared that the attacks "were not a clash of civilizations but a blow by a fanatical group on civilized societies in general." So, it is *not* an attack on the United States or its policies, but an attack on the West – on "civilized societies in general."

However, if this is not *the* clash, it will come in due time. In his book, *The Clash of Civilizations*, Huntington insists that our problem is not Islamic fundamentalism. "It is Islam, a different civilization whose people are convinced of the superiority of their culture and are obsessed with the inferiority of their power." On the other hand, the problem for Islamdom is not US policies: it is the West, whose people are "convinced of the universality of their culture and believe that their superior, if declining, power imposes on them the obligation to extend that culture throughout the world."[2] The clash is inevitable.

Are we to accept Huntington's reading of September 11 as an attack on the West, and part of an unfolding, or yet to begin, war between Islamdom and the West? I will show that if we eschew Bacon's 'idols' of the tribe and the market, and stay with the facts – some quite elementary facts – these theses become indefensible.

---

[2] Huntington (1998): 217.

First, consider the attacks of September 11 and place them alongside other attacks of a similar nature, of which they are an escalation. If we examine the history of such attacks – starting with the 1983 attacks on US interests in Lebanon, winding through more attacks on US embassies, military facilities, officials and citizens in Kuwait, Saudi Arabia, Yemen, Britain, Germany, Tanzania and Kenya, leading up to the culminating attacks of September 2001 – we have to face two unpleasant facts.

In nearly all cases, the target of these attacks was unmistakably the United States. It is also the case that in nearly every case, these attacks were carried out by Arabs, on Arab soil at first, but moving up to attacks in non-Arab countries and, eventually, to attacks on US soil. In the 1980s, the attackers were mostly Lebanese and Palestinians. Later, the Egyptians and Saudis joined their ranks.

What is the significance of these facts? First, they establish that the attackers were not waging war against "all civilized societies in general" but against *one* in particular – the United States – with less than one-third of the population of the West. Theirs is not a war against the West, or the freedom, democracy and pluralism of Western societies. It is also worth noting that the attacks were directed mostly against military and official targets. The exceptions are the Lockerbie crash and the two attacks on the World Trade Center. Equally important, nearly all the attackers were of Arab ethnicity; they have included few Pakistanis, Turks, Bangladeshis, Indonesians, Malays, Nigerians, Iranians or Afghans.

On two counts, then, we must reject the Huntington reading of the attacks of September 11. This and similar attacks have had a specific target, *viz.* the United States. Secondly, even if we regard the attackers as representative of Arab societies – a questionable assumption – this only pits one-sixth of the Islamicate world against less than one-third of the West. It would be a stretch to characterize this as a clash between two civilizations. Instead, this should help to focus our mind on US policies towards the Middle East.

We need to address another point. Huntington refers to Islam's "bloody borders" as evidence of a civilizational clash. Some might see these wars as proof of Islam's militant ethos. Just look at Bosnia, Chechnya, Palestine, Mindanao, Kosovo and Sinjiang; the Muslims are at war with everyone. On closer examination, however, this is in large part a result of Islam's geography and history. As recently as the seventeenth century, Islamic polities stretched in a nearly unbroken line from Mauritania to Mindanao. As Islam's political borders shrank over the next two centuries, several pockets of Muslim populations were left behind in non-Muslim states. Often persecuted and marginalized, these Muslims are now demanding greater autonomy or outright independence. Hence, the bloody borders.

Why then has the United States framed this conflict in terms of universals – as an attack on the West, on civilization itself? This language is well chosen. It serves a variety of goals. Most importantly, this rhetoric suppresses misgivings that the attacks of 9-11, causing 3,000 American deaths, were a blowback from our misconceived Middle East policies: the unconditional support of Israeli Occupation, propping corrupt and repressive dictatorships and monarchies in the Middle East and, not least, a policy of sanctions against Iraq that kills 5000 Iraqi children every month.

The language of an attack on "all civilized societies" – even as we avow our peaceful intentions towards Islamdom – evokes images of an attack by the Islamicate world against the West. It turns the focus away from the reality – of an attack by a handful of men who have turned to extreme methods to redress real and long-standing grievances. This has boosted the President's approval ratings to the mid-eighties, giving him a free hand in waging war, curtailing liberties and battening corporations.

This rhetoric helps to globalize America's new war against 'terror'. If September 11 can be packaged as an attack on "all civilized societies" – read, the West or Christendom – we can count on the atavistic passions this will arouse to bring Europe closer to the American position. Nevertheless, as we talk of extending the war beyond Afghanistan, to Sudan, Somalia and Iraq, many Europeans are beginning to break rank. Even Britain, a trusted ally, has been showing signs of nervousness.

None of this, however, implies that we *cannot* turn September 11 into a greater tragedy than it already is. It is tempting to leverage this event, wittingly or otherwise, into the clash of civilizations that Huntington predicts. We can do this by holding on to bases in Pakistan and Afghanistan, by pushing the war beyond Afghanistan, and by persecuting the Muslim population in the United States and eventually forcing their exodus. The Islamicate world will be watching what the United States does – more than they will be listening to what Americans say. As Americans – and world citizens – we should do everything we can to stop this human tragedy from turning into a disaster for humanity.

CHAPTER NINE

A Day that Changed America?

"The best Jihad is to speak the truth before a tyrannical ruler."

Muhammad[1]

December 17, 2002

In the aftermath of September 11, 2001, the fear, foreboding and outrage of many Americans was crystallized in a single phrase: it was "a day that changed America forever."

These words conveyed a tragic sense of loss, a sudden passage from innocence to grieving, a descent from security to susceptibility, an exit from exhilaration to angst. Suddenly, Americans, given to cruising at heavenly heights, had crash landed on terra firma; they faced terror in the heart of America. Momentarily, America had collided with the reality of a world mired in wars, poverty and disease; it had been struck by the shards of economies devastated, polities derailed, environments degraded by a rapacious globalization. In short, for one brief hour, America had glimpsed the agony endured for centuries by more than four-fifths of humanity, or what still goes by that name. It was as if, like Adam and Eve,

[1] Abū Dāwūd, *Sunan Abū Dāwūd*, II, 438, in: Mohammad Hashim Kamali, *Freedom of Expression in Islam* (Cambridge: Islamic Text Society, 1997): 11.

Americans had been expelled from Eden, banished from the land of perpetual bliss.

These wounds carried a revolutionary potential. Now that September 11 had rudely shattered Americans out of their cocooned bliss, ended their disconnection from the real world, they would avidly seek to expand their knowledge about its geography, history, politics and, most importantly, its peoples. They would ask not only about *who* had perpetrated the horrors of September 11, but *why*? They would not rest until they had answers to two troubling questions that delve into the origins, the logic and the genesis of September 11.

The first question concerns good and evil. Why had the 'goodness' of America been repaid by the evil of September 11? Many if not most Americans believe that they are a nation of do-gooders; that their country stands at the pinnacle of human evolution; it embodies better than any nation ever has the values of freedom and justice; it is a beacon of light to all mankind, fighting foreign tyrannies, propagating democracy, and sharing its own prosperity, ideas and technology with the world's less fortunate nations. *If* all this is indeed true, why did September 11 happen to us? Or, could it be that *we* have been duped, that the image of American munificence was just that, an image that concealed the reality of an ugly, imperialistic power like all others before?

The second question concerns the efficacy of America's vaunted military power. Americans know that their country is the only superpower, a distinction solidly built upon unrivalled economic strength, leadership in cutting-edge technologies, and an inestimably superior work force – advantages that allow the US government to gather intelligence worldwide, deploy troops worldwide, hit targets worldwide, and destroy incoming missiles before they can reach American shores. In short, they are convinced that they have the capacity to annihilate any country that dares to challenge them. However, none of this helped on September 11 when a handful of men, armed with nothing more lethal than box-cutters, attacked two venerable icons of American power, and within an hour killed some three thousand Americans, caused property damage worth tens of billions of dollars and still greater damage to the economy. Why was our government, they might well ask, spending 350 billion dollars a year on military hardware, troops, surveillance, intelligence and training if it could not stop nineteen men from "changing America forever?"

These are the questions that America's mass media might have asked after September 11 had they been free from corporate control. If the mass media had raised these questions, they would also be debated on college campuses, in churches, town halls and in the halls of the Congress. If this discourse could occur, it would slowly but surely effect a sea change in American perceptions about how their country projects its power overseas; about the ideals abandoned in our dealings with weaker nations; about our readiness to trample freedoms abroad, sacrifice non-American lives, and devastate entire economies in order to advance the corporate interests of a few Americans. If this discourse had occurred, Americans would finally wake up to the ugly realities of America abroad and mobilize – as they had mobilized against slavery and racial discrimination before – to force their government to pursue the same ideals abroad that it honors at home. If all this had indeed come to pass, then truly we could say that America had decisively defeated the perpetrators of September 11 – by changing America and the world for the better.

However, this is not how America changed after September 11. Americans could not be allowed to ask the *right* questions because this might lead them to the *wrong* answers – wrong, that is, for corporate America, for America's powerful oil interests, for the military establishment, for the Zionist lobby, for racists and for religious bigots. America's outrage over September 11 would not be answered by debate, discussion and dull inquiry. It would be placated by righteous indignation, by talk of evil antagonists, by promises of vengeance, by wars without end. America's grief would be hijacked by groups whose interests, security, power and profits batten on paranoia, bigotry, racism, wars and conflicts. Almost instantly, these forces responded to September 11 by orchestrating the deafening drumbeat of war. On September 11, Osama bin Laden had dared America. America obliged – with wars against Afghans and Palestinians, to be followed in time by wars against Iraqis, Iranians, Syrians, Saudis, Egyptians, Pakistanis and others.

President George Bush and his neoconservative warmongers took the lead in all this. They had found in the tragedy of September 11 the trigger for the war plans they had been hatching since the end of the Cold War in the early 1990s. Within days, George Bush *et al* had laid out their plans for global war before the American public. Even before the hijackers had been identified, they were linked to Al-Qaida, a "collection of loosely affiliated terrorist organizations." Their attacks were declared to be "an act of war against our country." This was no ordinary war, however. The Al-Qaida had launched a civilizational war; "they hate us," they are "enemies of freedom," they "hate our freedoms," they want to "disrupt and end a way of life." Al-Qaida's goal "is remaking the world—and imposing its radical beliefs on people everywhere." In other words, Al-Qaida wanted to impose their fundamentalist Islam on the United States and Europe.[2]

Wars spawn wars. So if Al-Qaida had started a war, the United States would have to respond in kind. The President declared that "the *only way* to defeat terrorism as a threat to our way of life is to

---

[2] All the quotes in this and the next paragraph are from President George Bush's speech of September 21, 2001, given to a joint session of Congress: www.guardian.co.uk/ Print/0,3858,4261868,00.html

stop it, eliminate it, and destroy it where it grows (emphasis added)." This global war "on terror begins with Al-Qaida, but it does not end there. It will not end until every terrorist group of global reach has been found, stopped and defeated." In time, this war will be extended to "nations that provide aid or safe haven to terrorism." In addition, this would not be a short war: it will be a "lengthy campaign, *unlike any we have ever seen* (emphasis added)." It will also be a total war, including "dramatic strikes, visible on TV, and covert operations, secret even in success." The Bush strategy was clear. Magnify the terrorist threat, fuel it, and prepare the nation for a war that would be global, total and unending.

Roma locuta est, causa finite est. President Bush had spoken, and the case was closed. All the organs of mainstream media concurred with Bush. The country was in the midst of a war, and it would tolerate nothing which carried a hint of dissent. Dissent was unpatriotic; some said it was treasonous. The Bush doctrine – you are against us if you are not with us – applied to individuals as well as states. The United States was now a country with one party, the party of Bush-Cheney-Rumsfeld-Ashcroft. Only the survivors of the victims of September 11 stuck to their demand for an independent investigation into September 11. When they persisted, the President reluctantly agreed, more than a year after September 11, to appoint an Independent Commission. Yet, in choosing Henry Kissinger to chair this Commission, the President ensured that it would be ineffectual. As one commentator quipped, he had put Dracula in charge of the blood bank.

Even without Kissinger to chair it, the Independent Commission on September 11 is unlikely to deliver any surprises. Its mandate only demands that it identify the factors that *allowed* the attacks on WTC and Pentagon to occur. The Commission will not hold any hearings in Grozny or Gaza, in Baghdad or Basra, in Kashmir or

Kabul, in Cairo or Karachi, in Jakarta or Jeddah, in Caracas or Kolkata, in Nairobi or Nouakchott. The Commission will not enter into the world of the hijackers; it will not probe into their lives, their grievances; it will not ask why the hijackers took their own lives to take American lives; it will not ask why the hijackers did not deliver their message by less violent means.

Presumably, all these questions had been answered definitively by Bush *et al.* The perpetrators of September 11 were evil, who acted from ineradicable spite, from a nihilistic rage against the modern world, against all that America represents, her freedom, democracy, progress and prosperity. After these incontestable answers, there was only one thing that remained to be done. Send the stealth bombers, cruise missiles, daisy-cutters and bunker-busting nukes to exorcise these demons.

Now, more than a year after that tragic morning on September 11 when nearly three thousand Americans were consumed in an inferno that descended from the skies, after all the rubble from the Ground Zero and the Pentagon has been cleared, can we say that America has changed forever? Did America embrace the potential for change contained in that terrible moment, the potential to connect with the inverse of our own world, a world whose sufferings, whose tyrannies, whose pathologies are deeply connected to ours in ways unknown to us? Were we overwhelmed by the slow dawning of the burden we bear, as the vanguard of the human enterprise, as the champions of Christian charity, to do something – even a little bit – to enrich, empower, enlighten and embrace those left behind? If Americans had taken up this challenge, if we *could* take up this challenge, then we would have turned a corner – and *that* would be a departure from old ways of doing things.

Instead, the captains of capital, the marshals of mass media, the total, global and unending to stop Americans from demanding change and to stop the rest of the world from getting the changes they deserve. As the wounds of global capitalism deepen, as the dark satanic mills of capitalist greed grind more than half of mankind deeper into poverty, as entire continents are devastated, as agro-corporations seek to chain millions of farmers to terminator seeds, as the middle classes in the rich countries slowly sink into poverty, as the consciousness of these depredations finally threatens to become global, the concentrated power of capital seized upon September 11 to divert Americans with gladiatorial combats on a global scale.

Let the drums of the news networks roll, let the combats begin, let blood be spilled daily, let entire countries be depopulated, let us convert mass extermination into a spectator sport. Let us sit back in our living rooms with Coke and Budweiser, and watch the greatest country in the world notch miraculous military victories over dictatorships that we had commissioned to murder their own people. Let us take deep draughts of sweet revenge. Only death will bring life, the death of all our enemics. Only devastation will bring peace. Only by these paradoxes will America be redeemed.

CHAPTER TEN

Why 9-11 and Why Now?

"*Our Lord! Bring us forth from out this town of which the people are oppressors! Oh, give us from Thy presence some protecting friend! Oh, give us from Thy presence some defender.*"

Qur'ān: 4: 75

"... *no other conquering nation has ever treated savage owners of the soil with such generosity as has the United States.*"

Theodore Roosevelt (1889)[1]

"*All told, the North American Indian population ... which had probably numbered in excess of twelve million in the year 1500, was reduced by official estimates to barely more than 237,000 four centuries later.*"

Ward Churchill (1994)[2]

December 17, 2002

If the attacks of September 11, 2001 are indeed 'unique,' without precedent in the long history of Western contacts with the 'lesser breeds', it is important that we make an effort to

[1] Theodore Roosevelt, *The Winning of the West, Vol. 4* (New York: Putnam, 1889): 54.

[2] Ward Churchill, *Indians Are Us* (Common Courage Press, 1994): http://web.mit.edu/ thistle/www/v9/9.11/1columbus.html

understand why they happened now, and what they say about our world?

The uniqueness of September 11 is not hard to establish. If we accept the officially sanctioned definition of terrorism, which restricts the term to violence directed against civilians by non-state actors, the attacks of September 11 gain a unique place in history because of their deadly human toll, some three thousand lives. On the other hand, these attacks pale into insignificance when compared to the civilian carnage perpetrated by states, not excluding the United States, over the past five hundred years.

A second claim to 'uniqueness' concerns the methods employed by the attackers. They had not employed guns, explosives, bombs or missiles. Instead, so we have been told, their weapons consisted of box-cutters and plastic knives. Armed with these, and their determination to die *with* their victims, the hijackers had flown civilian jets into the Twin Towers and the Pentagon. The German composer, Karlheinz Stockhausen, carried away by the power of the moment, described the self-immolation of these terrorists as "the greatest work of art ever." Later, retracting under pressure, he described the destruction as "Lucifer's greatest work of art."[3]

President Bush presented the third claim to 'uniqueness.' In his first address after September 11 to the members of Congress, he pointed out that "Americans have known wars – but for the past 136 years, they have been wars on foreign soil, except for one Sunday in 1941. Americans have known the casualties of war – but

[3] "Attacks Called Great Art," *The New York Times*, September 19, 2001, p. E3; and Kirsty Scott, "September 11 Apology by Hirst," *The Guardian*, September 20, 2002: www. guardian.co.uk/arts/news/story/0,11711,795385,00.html.

not at the center of a great city on a peaceful morning."[4] In other words, the attacks of September 11 were the first foreign assault against an American city after 1812.

Noam Chomsky offered a different take on the uniqueness of September 11. This was a "terrible terrorist atrocity," he wrote, but it was "not unique in scale, by any means." "What's unique about it, is the victims. This is the first time in hundreds of years that what we call the West – Europe and its offshoots – have been subjected to the kinds of atrocities that they carry out all the time in other countries and that is unique. The guns are pointed in the other direction for the first time."[5] The Indian writer and activist, Arundhati Roy, sums this up in a striking metaphor. The attacks of September 11, she wrote, "were a monstrous calling card from a world gone horribly wrong."[6]

Since 1492 the West has been on the offensive. For five hundred years now, the steel of their sword, lance, gun and bomb has been planted in the bones and flesh of Africans, Australians, Asians and Native Americans. For five hundred years, the Western powers divided the world into two unequal moieties, one planted on top of the other, one rising as the other sinks, one battening as the other sickens. For five hundred years, entire continents were devastated, societies overthrown, their civilizations denigrated, and their peoples subjugated, herded into slavery and stranded without dignity. All this

---

4 "Text of George Bush's Speech," *Guardian*, September 21, 2001: www.guardian.co.uk/ Print/0,3858,4261868,00.html.

5 "Noam Chomsky: Interview by Chris Spannos," www.vcn.bc.ca/ red-eye/interviews/ chomsky. html.

6 Arundhati Roy, "The Algebra of Infinite Justice," *The* Guardian, September 21, 2001: www.guardian.co.uk/Print/0,3858,4266289,00.html.

was the product of a new dynamic that welded power and capital, states and markets, in a cumulative process that divided the world into a dominant Core and a dependent Periphery, giving birth to unequal development, the inequalities growing cumulatively. Once it had been set in motion, this process could not be overthrown.

For five hundred years, the non-Western societies retreated, vacating their political, economic and cultural space before the surge of Western power. It must be asserted, however, that they never retreated without a fight; they fought against constantly increasing odds; they hid in ambush after every defeat; they stole the weapons of their enemies; after every defeat, they plotted and mobilized for the next battle. On many occasions, they stalled the advance of Western arms; they even won a few stunning victories. Finally, the tide began to turn with the Russian Revolution of 1917 and the Turkish success in repelling European invaders from the Anatolian peninsula in 1923. Slowly, the liberation movements began to gather momentum. Then, starting in the 1940s, with the colonial empires in retreat, the Periphery began to win back some breathing space.

Yet never in all these years could the victims attack their tormentors on their home turf, in their fortified playgrounds, inside the lavish retreats where they enjoyed the spoils of their conquests. Not once in all these years could the victims carry their resistance into the citadel of their oppressors. Though many peoples were crushed over these dim centuries, though many were driven into extinction, though many more were sold into slavery, though proud empires were laid waste, though ancient cultures were cast aside, not once could the victims breach the bastions, scale the citadels of Western power. Not once could the millions of Americans, Africans and Asians, whose lives were trapped in fear for centuries, bring fear to the homes of their tormentors. Inside their homelands, the captains of plunder were safe, beyond the reach of the wrath and the retribution of their countless victims.

September 11, 2001, changed that. On this fateful day, the victims had scaled the citadel of Western power, they had breached the impenetrable defense shield of the world's greatest power, they had cut through its security perimeter, and visited destruction inside its inner sanctum. On September 11, it would appear that the victims had desecrated the holy of holies. They had attacked two of the most visible icons of American financial and military power.

Do these attacks mark a turning of the tide? Do they mark the beginning of a new form of guerilla warfare, one that will be fought on the home turf of the United States? Did these attacks result from some new vulnerability created by changing technologies, the new connectivity between continents, or the new globalization? Were these attacks allowed to happen? Are they a new 'Operation Northwoods' executed surreptitiously by some cabal in the centers of power? Or are they flukes, a one-time disaster, the result of a momentary lapse in the defenses of the world's greatest power?

There are questions too about the attackers, their identity and their motives. Did they represent America's victims in Cuba, Haiti, Congo, Vietnam, Cambodia, Nicaragua, El Salvador, the Philippines, Afghanistan and Iraq? Had they acted out of sympathy for the victims of the United States and Israel in Palestine? Were they announcing their revulsion against the immorality of a world which allows tens of millions of children to die before they reach their fifth birthday, a world which now supports a growing trade in body parts? Are they Jehadists acting out of an atavistic faith which seeks to revive its glory by the force of arms? Or are they nihilists, rebels, madmen, deranged by the advance of modernity, by genetic engineering, terminator seeds, surrogate motherhood, designer children, stem-cell research and human cloning?

The answers to these questions – and many more like these – could have filled the pages of America's storied newspapers and magazines for many months. But theirs editors and columnists serve corporate masters; they cheer America's overseas wars; they think no sacrifice of foreign lives too great for advancing the profits of corporate America; they sanctify the crimes of a racist, expansionist, colonial-settler state; they can discover few virtues, little worth preserving outside the borders of their own great country. America's mass media works to ensure that no idea that can compromise the interests of corporate America ever enters the mind of Americans.

Was September 11 then a fluke, a contrived event, a shard from the past, history catching up with the amorality of power, the result of a new dynamic created by globalization and a new connectivity? Alternatively, should we accept the official answer, and see the hijackers of September 11 only as evil men, cold-blooded murderers, acting out of malicious spite, products of a failing civilization? Do we have the right to think, to evaluate, to empathize, to imagine, to choose? Do we dare to resist the machinery that manufactures consent?

In the world of social dynamics, few events are so simple that they can be traced back definitively to a single cause, as if we were examining not a social phenomenon but a disease that is carried by a single vector, a single malevolent life form that can then be destroyed with antibiotics. Should we ignore the complexity of the real world, the layers of causation, the interconnections amongst humans – even between tormentors and their victims – and reach for convenient answers, answers that exonerate us, answers that invert reality, even transforming villains into heroes, tormentors into victims? Sadly, that is what our media and academia do, because they are beholden to money and power.

We might assert, and quite accurately, that September 11 happened because of skyscrapers: the attacks would never have occurred if the 'monstrous' Twin Towers did not exist. If our media were dominated by interests inimical to tall buildings – for reasons of aesthetics, economics or politics – this is the explanation that would have prevailed. The solution too would have been simple: level America's skyline. We would have created a wrecker's paradise, a boom for demolition companies.

Alternatively, we might argue that the culprits were the passenger jets. Who can deny that these jets were the instruments of destruction chosen by the hijackers? The hijackers had used no cluster bombs, no cruise missiles, no daisy-cutters; they had simply turned these flying behemoths into massive weapons. "Ban commercial air travel," the cry could have gone up. In fact, this solution did make sense in the immediate aftermath of the attacks, when the United States grounded all commercial flights for a few days. It was a sensible thing to do. However, if the anti-airline lobbies had been powerful we would have grounded them permanently and gone back to traveling the old-fashioned way – by ships and trains.

It is appropriate, however, that the search into the causes of September 11 began with the perpetrators of these attacks. Very quickly the nineteen dead hijackers were identified; we learned that they were male, young, Arab and Islamic. Once this identification had been made, a great deal of the surmise, analysis, investigation and response turned on the Arab-Islamic ethnicity of the hijackers. For many commentators, especially those with Zionist proclivities or evangelical vocations, this singular fact contained all the answers. The hijackers were messengers of death from the Arab-Islamic hell. For years, these fiends had brought death to innocent Israelis. And now they have directed their terror against the free, democratic and Christian West itself. Their hatred of the West has no political causes, no political grievances and no history: it springs from their race, their ethos, and their devilish, war-mongering creed.

This line of thinking led to some quick solutions. Ann Coulter, contributing editor of *National Review Online*, proposed, "We should invade their countries, kill their leaders and convert them to Christianity."[7] The solution appeared eminently logical. Since the Islamicate world is the source of terrorism, the United States should exorcise Islam, exterminate the Muslims or convert them to Christianity. That done, we can have peace and goodwill on earth. Although this may sound outlandish, the United States has been moving in this general direction since September 11. Already, we have invaded Afghanistan and are getting ready to invade Iraq in what promises to be the first leg of a plan of Middle Eastern conquests that will take us to Iran, Syria, Saudi Arabia and Egypt. After that, the sky is the limit.

There was another solution that the United States began implementing right after September 11, 2001. It is a solution in which it has long experience: racial profiling. Once again, the solution appeared logical. All nineteen hijackers were young Arab men. If the United States could get tough on Arabs, keep tabs on them, track them, screen them at the border, arrest them on suspicion, abridge

---

[7] Ann Coulter, "This Is War," *National Review Online*, September 13, 03: www.nationalreview.com/coulter/coulter091301.shtml

their civil rights, all Americans could sleep in peace. This might just work if the terrorists are only capable of *repeating* September 11. What if the team Al-Qaida is recruiting even now includes Italian, Greek, Hispanic or Chinese Muslims? Should the United States extend racial profiling to these new groups? How will this affect the corporate project of globalization?

Why did corporate and official America – the America projected by our mass media – respond to September 11 by reverting to old stereotypes? Americans are the knights in shining armor, once again slaying the dragons that had dared to breathe fire over their cities. Once again, they are battling the slovenly Arabs, the violent Muslims, the fanatic Orientals. At the dawn of the twenty-first century, the world's most advanced country is mobilizing for the modern world's first civilizational war. If this war unfolds according to plans – and when the plans begin to unravel – the memory of the Crusades might pale in comparison. That was a local war fought in one sector of the Islamicate world. Already this new war is being fought on a broader front that includes Afghanistan, Palestine, Iraq and Philippines. And it threatens to be a great deal more deadly.

In the 1990s, following the collapse of Soviet Union, two visions competed to shape America's dominance in the world. The first was the project of globalization. It strove to open up world markets to American capital, every corner of the world, including the Third World and the former communist countries. In the past, Europe had achieved this through force of arms, but even so it was incomplete. Now the United States could do a great deal more, without waging too many wars, without creating a formal empire. Instead, it would use its dominating presence in the global economy – backed no doubt by its unchallenged military might – to define the rules of the global economy, rules that would open up the world, as never before, to the free entry of American capital. This was the vision that dominated throughout the 1990s.

However, the hawks would have their day. The contradictions of globalization would bring this about. As globalization advanced, it deepened poverty in large sections of the Periphery, transferred jobs out of the Core countries, augmented the power of Corporations, and threatened the environment. Together, these developments produced a new countervailing force – an anti-globalization movement that was itself global. Driven by the same connectivity that was driving globalization, anti-globalization became global. By the late 1990s, anti-globalization posed a serious challenge to the corporate elites and their globalization project. At its edges the movement contained radical tendencies. Anti-globalization had to be contained.

Another imperial project was running into trouble. In May 2000, the Israelis beat a hasty retreat from South Lebanon, changing the mood of the Palestinian resistance, and forcing Arafat to reject the Bantustans offered by Israelis in July 2000. Three months later, the second Intifada was born, forcing the Likudniks and their American allies – the neoconservative hawks – to turn to their second option that was aimed at the ethnic cleansing of Palestinians from the West Bank. This plan called for the entry of the United States itself into a war against the Arabs. At some point in the course of this war, it would be safe to drive the Palestinians out of the West Bank. In May 2002, Dick Armey, the House Republican Majority Leader, proposed to "transfer" the Palestinians to the deserts of Western Iraq.[8]

---

[8] "Rep. Dick Armey Calls for Ethnic Cleansing of Palestinians," *Counterpunch. Org*, May 2, 2002: http://www.counterpunch.org/armey0502.html.

A third force was also brewing in the United States. It was the force of the religious right, the Christian Coalition: they hark back to the letter of the Bible, they read the old prophecies into modern history, and their worldview is Manichean. They are mostly Southerners and racists, who want America to launch a new Crusade against the Islamicate world. More importantly, they have been plotting to take over the Republican Party. And in 2000, they were already a major force in the Presidential election.

In the meanwhile, the neoconservative hawks also plotted. In a "Statement of Principles," announced in June 1997, they laid out plans for '*The New American Century*,' an imperial century that would "increase defense spending significantly," "shape circumstances before crises emerge," "meet threats before they become dire," and "challenge regimes hostile to our interests and values."[9] In another document, published in September 2000, these neoconservatives complain that the "process of transformation" they wanted to effect "is likely to be a long one, absent some catastrophic and catalyzing event – like a new Pearl Harbor."[10]

Was September 11 the "catastrophic and catalyzing event" without which the neoconservatives could scarcely launch their '*New American Century*?' Was it the inevitable escalation in a clash of civilizations, another twist in the unfolding inner logic of the Zionist project, or a symptom of a deepening crisis in the relations between

---

[9] The words in quotes are from the "The Statement of Principles," showcased on the website of *The Project For The New American Century*, signed by the major neoconservatives, including Dick Cheney, Donald Rumsfeld, Elliot Abrams, Paul Wolfowitz, Norman Podhoretz, I. Lewis Libby and Eliot Cohen. See www.newamericancentury.org/statementofprinciples.htm

[10] Tom Barry and Jim Lobe, "The Men Who Stole the Show," *Foreign Policy In Focus*, October 2002: www.fpif.org/papers/02men/box1_body.html.

the Core and Periphery? Was it serendipity, conspiracy or kismet that produced these fateful attacks? Perhaps, it was all of the above.

Whatever the forces that engineered September 11, this much is clear. It was seized precipitately by the quartet just described – the American Likudniks, Corporate America, the Zionists and the Christian Coalition – to launch their project of a '*New American Century*,' to proclaim endless wars, to seize the profits from the Arab oil fields, to shrink and downsize Islamdom, to make the world safe for American interests, and to create a hegemony that would last forever. Do we indeed stand at the dawn of a new American Century, whose birth threatens the world with wars, blood, grime, but also promises to deliver profits never dreamed of before?

A hundred years from now, standing in front of the majestic monuments raised to commemorate this grand American century, what will Americans think of Osama bin Laden? Will they remember this malevolent genius as the midwife who facilitated the birth of '*The New American Century*?' On the other hand, if this project runs into trouble, if it produces blood and grime but no profits, who shall we blame for the human toll of this terrible catastrophe? We can of course blame bin Laden. Or, smitten by conscience, we can blame the cold hearts, minds cowed by fear, grasping cupidity and a terrible tribalism that delivered humankind, gagged and bound, into the power of the neoconservative Juggernaut.

CHAPTER ELEVEN

Iraq is Free

"*It is most hateful in the sight of Allah that ye say that which ye do not.*"

Qur'ān: 61: 3

Leslie Stahl: "*We have heard that half a million children have died. I mean, that's more children than died in Hiroshima. And you know, is the price worth it?*"

Madeleine Albright: "*I think this is a very hard choice, but the price - we think the price is worth it.*"

CBS, *Sixty Minutes*, May 12, 1996

March 11, 2003

Iqra, recite, proclaim, affirm, avow, declare: *Iraq is free.*

Iraq has been freed from ten thousand years of tyranny; freed from darkest infamy; freed from cold villainy; freed from centuries of stasis; freed from nights of searing pain; freed from terrible torture; freed from sanctioned starvation; freed from laser-guided precision; freed from bombs that explode with shock and awe.

The whole world was witness to this historical moment. They saw the dark head of the tyrant, the granite head of Ozymandias draped in the fabric of freedom, effaced, his sneer blotted out, his terror nullified, brought down by the force of an armor-clad Bradley vehicle. Iraqis, many dozens of them, cheered lustily. A few even kissed the liberators on both cheeks, in authentic Arab style.

The naysayers, skeptics, doubting Thomases, pacifists, prophets of doom, and the patriotically challenged were wrong about America's war *in* Iraq. The millions who marched in the streets, protesting the war, are now gnashing their teeth. In deep shame, penitent, they have announced that they will march again in the millions, to curse, flog and flagellate themselves for marching *against* the war that freed Iraqis.

This was not a war *on* Iraq, much less a war *against* Iraq. It was a war *in* Iraq: a war *for* the Iraqis. It was not the first time that a great civilizing nation has fought a war *in* a barbarous land *against* its homegrown tyrants. Civilized nations have carried this burden uncomplainingly, showing equal dedication in freeing lands *of* their peoples and, when the occasion demanded, freeing peoples *of* their lands. The United States now carries the torch of freedom, bravely torching anyone who shows the gall to oppose the forward march of the brave and free.

Consider the freedoms this war has bestowed on Iraq.

First, this war has freed Iraq of its WMDs. It is not surprising if the Americans have not yet found any caches of WMDs inside Iraq: the experts knew this all along. In the days leading up to the war, the WMDs were smuggled into Syria for safekeeping. However, this only means that Americans will have to go the extra mile, into Syria. In time, Syria will smuggle the WMDs into Egypt, Egypt into Libya, Libya into Iran, and Iran into Sudan. Is this an Arab conspiracy – or what – to hitch a freedom ride on Bradleys and Abrams tanks?

Instantly, the American liberators have turned the Iraqis free to pillage their museums, strip their hospitals, plunder their universities, and loot their homes. The acutely funny Donald Rumsfeld explained: "It's untidy. And freedom's untidy. And free people are free to make mistakes and commit crimes and do bad things." Quickly, the Iraqis are learning that the gift of freedom comes at a price. They are eager to prove that their freedom is worth the price they are being asked to pay for it. If Madeline Albright could sacrifice the lives of half a million Iraqi children for *American* security, surely the Iraqis can give up their national treasures for a fleeting taste of freedom.

The war has freed Iraq to spread the welcome mat to American Corporations. For thirteen long years, since Gulf War I, American capital was not free to fertilize the Iraqi economy; this was an unconscionable abridgement of freedom. Now, the playing fields have been leveled. The Bechtels, Halliburtons, Northrops, Exxons and Triremes are free at last to claim their pound of Iraqi flesh.

There is good news too for the pastoral faction of American capital, for outfits like Franklin Graham's Good Samaritans. After years of softening with sanctions and bombings, their would-be-victims are free to receive the good word of the Lord. Even as I write, the Samaritan convoys are converging on Iraq, ready to trade American food and water for Iraqi souls. The Iraqis never knew a better bargain, getting something for nothing.

Iraq is now free, as Egyptians freed themselves after suffering the fourth defeat at the hands of Israel in 1973, to derive the inestimable benefits of 'normal' relations with Israel. After 55 years, Iraqi oil is now free again to flow to Haifa. In addition, Iraqi water too is free to flood the parched swimming pools in Israel and the West Bank settlements.

Freed from the threat of Iraq's WMDs, Israelis can now attack the Palestinian problem – the Palestinian menace in Judea and Samaria – with impunity. The pace of ethnic cleansing, too slow for an early final solution, can now be accelerated. Now that Iraq is free, with Americans in charge of its land and resources, it should be relatively easy teleporting the Palestinians to the deserts of Western Iraq.

The war has freed another Arab capital from the threat of Israel's Samson option. Once the unimpeded looting of their hospitals, universities and museums stops, the five million citizens of Baghdad can sleep in peace. Never again will they be troubled by nightmares of being incinerated in a nuclear inferno. Sanctions, wars and occupation are but a small price to pay for the inestimable gift of an Iraq free from Israeli threats of a nuclear holocaust.

If one counts all the advantages of America's war *in* Iraq – and I have barely started – history will record that this war created the greatest opening in Iraqi history, a greater moment than the first founding of civilization on the banks of Tigris and Euphrates. Once the Iraqis wake to this shattering truth, they will also acknowledge their deep debt to Saddam Hussein. Without his anti-Zionism, his methodical recklessness, his development of WMDs, his support for terrorism, and his financing of Al Qaida, the United States would never have waged a war to liberate Iraq. Without Saddam Hussein, the Iraqis would still be toiling under some vapid dictator, allied to Israel and receiving bribes from the United States. I can imagine a day, once the fog of America's war *in* Iraq clears, when repentant Iraqis may restore Saddam Hussein's statue to the high pedestal it had long occupied in Baghdad's Central Square. In shock and awe, these are the words that American visitors will read inscribed on its base:

Saddam Hussein
A Brave Iraqi
Serendipitous Architect of Our Freedoms

CHAPTER TWELVE

Dialectics of Terror

"If you kill one person, it is murder. If you kill a hundred thousand, it is foreign policy."

Anonymous

August 7, 2003

States are founded on a monopoly over violence; this is their very essence. They enforce this monopoly by amassing instruments of violence; but that is scarcely enough. They also use religion, ideology and laws to de-legitimize and exorcise violence by non-state agents.

This monopoly over violence creates its own problems. Unchallenged, the state can direct violence against its own population. This leads to state tyranny. The state can also wage wars to enrich one or more sectional interests. This defines the dual challenge before all organized societies: restraining state tyranny and limiting its war-making powers.

Often, a trade off exists between state tyranny and wars. Arguably, such a tradeoff was at work during the period of European expansion – since the sixteenth century – when Europeans slowly secured political rights even as they engaged in growing, even genocidal, violence, especially against non-Europeans. As Western states gradually conceded rights to their own populations, they intensified the murder and enslavement of Amerindians and Africans, founding white colonies on lands stolen from them. This inverse connection troubled few Westerners: it was the essence of racism.

The United States is only the most successful of the colonial creations; and this has left an indelible mark on American thinking. It was founded on violence against its native inhabitants, who were pushed to near-extinction to accommodate the growing tide of European immigrants. Its history also includes the violence – on a nearly equal scale – perpetrated against the Africans who were torn from their continent to create wealth for the new Republic. Such a genesis, steeped in violence against other races, convinced most Americans that they had the divine right – like the ancient Israelites – to build their prosperity on the ruin of other, inferior races.

This racism goes a long way to explain why so many Americans give blind support to their government's interventions abroad. It is unnecessary – they might be saying – to look too closely into these interventions; after all, they *are* undertaken to secure 'our' interests. Even if these interventions result in deaths – the deaths of more than three-quarters of a million children, as in Iraq – most Americans keep a clear conscience about these deaths. In the felicitous phrase of Madeline Albright, the US Secretary of State, they know that "the price is worth it."

Few Americans understand that their country has long stood at the apex – and, therefore, is the chief beneficiary – of a global system that produces poverty for the greater part of humanity; that this system subordinates all social, cultural, environmental and human values to the imperatives of corporate capital; a system that now kills millions merely by setting trade, investment and property regimes that devastate their economies, deprive them of their livelihood, their dignity and, eventually, their lives. The corporate media, the school curricula, and the Congress ensure that most Americans never see past the web of deceit – about a free, just, tolerant and caring United States – that covers up the human carnage and environmental wreckage this system produces.

The wretched of the earth are not so easily duped. They can see – and quite clearly, through the lens of their dark days – how corporate capital, with the United States in the lead, produces their home-based tyrannies; how their economies have been devastated to enrich transnational corporations and their local collaborators; how the duo stifle indigenous movements for human rights, women's rights and worker's rights; how they devalue indigenous traditions and languages; how their countries are used as markets, as sources of cheap labor, as fields for testing new, deadlier weapons, and as sites for dumping toxic wastes; how their men and women sell body parts because the markets place little value on their labor.

The world – outside the dominant West – has watched how the Zionists, with the support of Britain and the United States, imposed a historical anachronism, a colonial-settler state in Palestine, a throwback to a racist past, when indigenous populations in the Americas could be cleansed with impunity to make room for Europe's superior races. In horror, the world watches daily how a racist Israel destroys the lives of millions of Palestinians through US-financed weaponry and fresh-contrived acts of malice; how it attacks its neighbors at will; how it has destabilized, distorted and derailed the historical process in an entire region; and how, in a final but foreordained twist, American men and women have now been drawn into this conflict, to make the Middle East safe for Israeli hegemony.

In Iraq, over the past thirteen years, the world has watched the United States showcase the methods it will use to crush challenges to the new imperialism – the New World Order – that was launched after the end of the Cold War. This new imperialism commands more capital and more lethal weapons than the old imperialisms of Britain, France or Germany. It is imperialism without rivals and, therefore, it dares to pursue its schemes, its wars, and its genocidal campaigns, under the cover of international legitimacy, through the United Nations, the World Bank, IMF and World Trade Organization. In brief, it is a deadlier, more pernicious imperialism.

Under the cover of the Security Council, the United States has waged a total war against Iraq, a war that went well beyond the means that were necessary to reverse the invasion of Kuwait. The aerial bombing of Iraq, in the months preceding the ground action in January 1991, sought to destroy the country's civilian infrastructure, a genocidal act under international law; it destroyed power plants, water-purification plants, sewage facilities, bridges and bomb shelters. It was the official (though unstated) aim of these bombings to sting the Iraqis into overthrowing their rulers. Worse, the war was followed by a never-relenting campaign of aerial bombings and the most rigorous sanctions in recorded history. According to a UN study, the sanctions had killed half a million Iraqi children by 1995, the result of a five-fold increase in child mortality rates. It would have taken five Hiroshima bombs to produce this grisly toll.

Then came September 11, 2001, a riposte from the black holes of global capitalism to the New World Order. Nineteen hijackers took control of passenger airplanes in Boston, Newark and Virginia, and rammed them, one after another, into the twin towers of the Word Trade Center and the Pentagon; the fourth missed its target, possibly the White House. Following a carefully rehearsed script, the nineteen hijackers enacted a macabre ritual, taking their own lives even as they took the lives of nearly three thousand Americans. The hijackers did not wear uniforms; they were not flying stealth bombers; they carried nothing more lethal (so we are told) than box cutters and plastic knives; they had not been dispatched or financed by any government. Nevertheless, using the principles of jujitsu, they had turned the civilian technology of the world's greatest power against its own civilians. As Arundhati Roy put it, the hijackers had delivered "a monstrous calling card from a world gone horribly wrong."[1]

The terrorist attacks of 9-11 shocked, perhaps traumatized, a whole nation. Yet the same Americans expressed little concern – in fact, most could profess total ignorance – about the hundreds of thousands of dead Iraqis, a horrendous toll exacted by daily bombings and crippling sanctions over a period of thirteen years. Of course, the dollar and the dinar are not the same. American deaths cannot be placed side by side with Iraqi deaths. The Iraqis were after all evil; they harbored ill will towards the United States. And evil people should never be given a chance to repent or change their evil-doing propensities. Senator John McCain said it succinctly: "We're coming after you. God may have mercy on you, but we won't."[2]

The simultaneous attacks of 9-11 required a high level of planning, training and skill. On this ground, some argued that it could not have been the work of "incompetent" Arabs. However, it would appear that there is greater political cunning at work in the conception of these attacks. Al-Qaida delivered what the Bush hawks wanted, a terrorist attack that would inflame Americans into supporting a war against the Arabs. In turn, the Bush hawks gave what the Al-Qaida wanted, a war that would plant tens of thousands of Americans in the cities and towns of the Islamicate world.

The attacks of September 11, 2001, represented massive failures of intelligence and security in a country that spends tens of billions of dollars annually on intelligence gathering and hundreds of billions

---

[1] Arundhati Roy, "The Algebra of Infinite Justice," *The* Guardian, September 21, 2001: www.guardian.co.uk/Print/0,3858,4266289,00.html.

[2] John Diamond and Bob Kemper, "Bush Lining Up Allies for Retaliation," *Chicago Tribune, September 13, 2001*: http://www.chicagotribune.com/news/specials/911/showcase/ chi-warinafghanistan,0,1468693.story.

more on its military. It should have led to an immediate Congressional inquiry; in fact, this would not start for another year. Instead, President Bush declared that 9-11 was an act of war (making it the first act of war perpetrated by nineteen civilians), and proceeded to declare unlimited war against terrorists (also the first time that war had been declared against elusive non-state actors). In the name of a bogus war against terrorism, the United States appropriated the right to wage preemptive wars against any country suspected of harboring terrorists or possessing weapons of mass destruction (what are weapons for if not mass destruction?) with an intent (US would be the judge of that) to use them against the United States.

Osama bin Laden had the victory that he wanted: the world's only superpower was running mad after him and his cohorts. Al-Qaida now occupied the place vacated by the Soviet Union. No terrorist organization could have asked for greater recognition, and this was almost certain to help in Al-Qaida's recruitment drive. Secondly, by declaring war against Al-Qaida, the United States had tied its own prestige to the daily casualties of this war. Every terrorist strike – the softer the target the better – would be counted by Americans and the rest of the world as a battle lost in the war against terrorism. It should come as no surprise that the frequency of large-scale terrorist strikes has increased markedly since 9-11 – from Baghdad to Bali and Bombay. Thirdly, President Bush's war against terrorism has already placed 160,000 American troops in Iraq and Afghanistan, not counting additional thousands in other Islamicate countries. Already, it would appear that Al-Qaida is capitalizing upon this opportunity to open a broad front against the United States on its home turf.

Although the Crusader presence in the Levant, starting in the 1090s, lasted for nearly two centuries, this did not provoke a pan-Islamic Jihad against the 'Infidels.' On occasion, some Muslim states formed alliances with the Crusaders to contain the ambitions of rival

Muslim states. It was only in 1187, after Salahuddin had united Syria and Egypt, that the Muslims took back Jerusalem. However, the Arabs did not carry their counter-attack to a decisive end; the Crusaders retained control of parts of coastal Syria for another hundred years. Indeed, several years later, Salahuddin's successors returned Jerusalem to the Crusaders on the condition that they would not fortify it. The Muslims did not look upon the Crusades, which loom so large in European imagination, as a civilizational war.

Of course, that was then, when Islamicate societies were prosperous, refined, tolerant, self-confident and strong. As a result, although the Crusades threw the combined might of Western Europe – that region's first united enterprise – to regain Christian holy lands, the Muslims took the invasions in their stride. Eventually, the resources of a relatively small part of the Muslim world were sufficient to end this European adventure, which left few lasting effects on the region. In the more recent past, Islamicate societies have been divided, fragmented, outstripped by their European adversaries, their states embedded in the periphery of the global economy, and their rulers allied with Western powers against their own people. This fragmentation of Islamdom is not a natural condition in the historical consciousness of Muslims.

More ominously, since 1917 the Arabs have faced settler-colonialism in their very heartland, an open-ended imperialist project successively supported by Britain and the United States. This Zionist insertion in the Middle East, self-consciously promoted as the outpost of the West in the Islamicate world, produced its own twisted dialectics. An exclusive Jewish state founded on fundamentalist claims (and nothing gets more fundamentalist than a twentieth-century imperialism founded on 'divine' promises about real estate made three thousand years back) was bound to evoke its counterpart in the Islamicate world. In 1967 when Israel inflicted a humiliating defeat on Egypt and Syria – the leading proponents of Arab nationalism – this created an opening for the insertion of Islamists into the region's political landscape. One fundamentalism would now be pitted against another.

This contest may now be reaching its climax – with the United States entering the war directly. In part at least, it is the unfolding of the logic of the Zionist insertion in the Arab world. On the one hand, this has provoked the growth of Islamist movements, some of which were forced by US-supported repression in their home countries to target the United States. On the other hand, the Zionist occupation of lands rich in Biblical lore has encouraged the growth of Christian Zionism, predicated on the conviction that all the Jews of the world must assemble in Israel before the Second Coming of Christ. At the same time, Zionist propagandists – based in America's think tanks, media and academia – have worked tirelessly to arouse old Western fears about Islam and Muslims. They paint Islam as a violent religion, perennially at war against infidels, opposed to democracy, fearful of women's rights, unable to modernize, and raging at the West for its freedoms and prosperity. They never tire of repeating that the Arabs hate Israel because it is the only 'democracy' in the Middle East.

Arguably, the US occupation of Iraq is in some trouble. Already, there has been a retreat from plans to bring about regime change in Iran, Syria, Saudi Arabia and Egypt. There is still talk of bringing democracy to Iraq and the Arab world, but it carries little conviction even with American audiences. There is new-fangled talk now of fighting the "terrorists" in Baghdad and Basra rather than in Boulder and Buffalo. Further, after two years of bristling unilateralism, the United States is back at the Security Council, imploring the world to share the financial and human costs of their occupation of Iraq. It is unlikely that Indians, Pakistanis or Egyptians will play human shield for American troops in Iraq. In any case, it is unlikely that any re-christening of the Occupation will fool the Iraqi resistance.

What can be the outcome of all this? During their long rampage through history, begun in 1492, the Western powers have shown little respect for the peoples they encountered in the Americas, Africa, Asia and Australia. Many of them are not around to recount the gory history of their extermination through imported diseases, warfare, and forced labor in mines and plantations. Those who survived were forced into peonage, or consigned to mutilated lives on reservations. Many tens of millions were bought and sold into slavery. Proud empires were dismembered. Great civilizations were denigrated. All this had happened before, but never on this scale. In part, perhaps, the extraordinary scale of these depredations may be attributed to what William McNeill calls the "deep-rooted pugnacity" of Europeans.[3] Much of this, however, is due to historical accidents which elevated West Europeans – rather than the Chinese, Turks or Indians – to great power based on their exploitation of inorganic sources of energy. If we are to apportion blame, we might as well award the prize to Britain's rich coal deposits.

In the period since the Second World War, some of the massive historical disequilibria created by Western powers have been corrected. China and India are on their feet; so are Taiwan, South Korea, Singapore, Hong Kong and Malaysia. These countries are on their feet and advancing. However, the wounds of imperialism in Africa run deeper. The colonial legacies of fragmented societies, deskilled populations, arbitrary boundaries, and economies tied to failing primary production continue to produce wars, civil wars, corruption, massacres and diseases. Yet, the West can ignore Africa; the deaths of a million Africans in the Congo do not merit the attention given to one suicide bombing in Tel Aviv. Africa can be ignored because its troubles do not affect vital Western interests; at least not yet.

---

[3] William H. McNeill, *The Rise of the West* (Chicago: University of Chicago Press, 1991).

Then there is the failure of the Islamicate world to reconstitute itself. As recently as 1700, three major Muslim empires – the Mughal, Ottoman and Safavid – together controlled the greater part of the Islamicate world. By 1800, after a period of rivalry among indigenous successor states and European interlopers, the Mughals had given way to the British in much of India. The Ottoman Empire disintegrated more slowly, losing Egypt and its European territories in the nineteenth century, and then during the First World War the remaining Arab territories were divvied up amongst the British, French, Zionists, Maronites and a clutch of oil-rich protectorates. The Iranians alone held on to most of the territories acquired by the Safavids. In short, the colonial onslaught had fragmented Islamdom, divided it into some forty states, none with the potential to serve as a core state; and this fragmentation was most striking in Islamdom's Arab heartland. In addition, significant Muslim populations now lived in states with non-Muslim majorities.

Why did the Muslims fail to reconstitute their power? Most importantly, this was because Muslim power lacked a demographic base. The Mughal Empire ruled over a non-Muslim majority; the Ottomans faced a similar situation in their European territories. More recently, the Muslims have been the victims of geological 'luck,' containing the world's richest deposits of oil, the fuel that drives the global economy. The great powers could not let the Muslims control *their* lifeblood. The Muslims suffered a third setback from a historical accident: the impetus that Hitler gave to the Zionist movement. Now there had emerged a powerful new interest – a specifically Jewish interest – in keeping the Arabs divided and dispossessed.

It appears, however, that Muslims have not acquiesced to their fragmentation or the capitulation of their governments to Anglo-Zionist power. We have watched the resilience of the Muslims, their determination to fight for their dignity in Afghanistan, Bosnia,

Palestine, Chechnya, Kashmir and Mindanao – among other places. In the meanwhile, they have overcome their demographic weakness. At the beginning of the twentieth century, the Muslims constituted barely a tenth of the world population; today that share already exceeds 23 percent, and continues to rise. Moreover, unlike the Chinese or Hindus, the Muslims inhabit a broad swathe of territory from Nigeria, Senegal and Morocco in the west to Sinjiang and the Indonesian Archipelago in the east. It would be hard to corral a population of this size that spans half the globe. More likely, the US-British-Israeli siege of the Islamicate world, now underway in the name of the war against terrorism, will lead to a broadening conflict with unforeseen consequences that could easily turn very costly for either or both parties.

Can the situation yet be saved? In the weeks before the launch of the illegal war against Iraq, when tens of millions of Europeans and Americans marched against the war, it appeared that the war-mongering 'democracies' could be stopped from executing their belligerent designs; that the marchers would defeat the ideologies of hatred and the tactics of fear-mongering; it appeared that if the demands for diplomacy were denied, the marchers would resort to civil disobedience to stop the carnage. However, once the war began, the protesters melted away like picnicking crowds when a sunny day is marred by rains. In retrospect, the protests lacked the depth, organization and grit to graduate into political movements. America does not easily stomach anti-war protestors once it *starts* a war. Wars are serious business. Once the killing begins, war must have the undivided support of the whole country. Support for the war becomes support for *our* troops.

The anti-war protesters may yet regroup, but not before many more body bags arrive in the continental United States, before many more young Americans are maimed for life, before many tens of thousands of Iraqis are dispatched to early deaths. Attempts are already underway to invent new lies to keep Americans deluded about the war; to tighten the noose around Iran; to hide the growing casualties of war; to lure poverty-stricken Mexicans and Guatemalans to die for America; to substitute Indian and Pakistani body bags for American ones. America's war mongering cannot be stopped unless *more* Americans can be taught to separate their government from their country, their leaders from their national interests, and their tribal affiliation from their humanity.

This can be done. We now posses a new medium – the internet – to create a new consciousness, to get past the mercenary media, the pusillanimous politicians, the spineless social scientists, the serenading schools, and putrid prejudices. If some of us had done a better job getting past these hurdles in time, the nineteen hijackers may never have delivered their monstrous calling card, and they and their three thousand victims might still be alive today. Still, the hijackers chose the wrong means to deliver their message; by targeting civilians, they played right into the game plan of the Bush hawks. The result has been more profits for favored US corporations, greater freedom of action for Israel, and more lives and liberties lost everywhere. At least, this is what the ledger of history shows for now.

CHAPTER THIRTEEN

Semantics of Empire

"*Saddam Hussein is a man who is willing to gas his own people ...*"

George Bush, March 22, 2002

"*As he (George Bush) said, any person that would gas his own people is a threat to the world.*"

Scott McClellan, White House spokesperson, March 31, 2002

"*Saddam Hussein is a tyrant who has tortured and killed his own people.*"

Hillary Clinton, October 10, 2002

"*He poison-gassed his own people.*"

Al Gore, December 16, 1998

December 24, 2003

We might glean a few insights about the semantics of the global order – and the reality it tries to mask – from the way in which the United States has framed the moral case against Saddam.

Saddam's unspeakable crime is that he has "tortured his *own* people." He has "killed his *own* people." He has "gassed his *own* people." He has "poison-gassed his *own* people." In all the accusations, Saddam stands inseparable from his *own* people.

Rarely do his accusers charge that Saddam "tortured people," "gassed people," "gassed Iraqis," or "killed Iraqis." A google search for "gassed his *own* people" and "Saddam" produced 5980 hits. Another search for "gassed people" and "Saddam" produced only 276 hits.

It would appear that the indictment of Saddam gathers power, conviction, irrefutability, by adding the possessive, proprietary, emphatic 'own' to the people tortured, gassed or killed. What does the grammar of accusations say about the metrics of American values?

It is revealing. For a country that claims to speak in the name of man, abstract man, universal man, the charge is not that Saddam has killed people, that he has committed murders, mass murders. Instead, the prosecution indicts him for killing a people who stand in a specific relation to the killer: they are his *own* people.

This betrays tribalism. It springs from a perception that fractures the indivisibility of mankind. It divides men into tribes. It divides people into "us" and "them:" "ours" and "theirs." It elevates "us" above "them:" "our" kind above "their" kind. It reveals a sensibility that can feel horror only over the killing of one's *own* kind.

Life is sacred at the Core. In the United States, *we* have an inalienable right to life. It is protected by law; it cannot be taken away without due process. Americans are proud, sedate, in the illusion that *their* President never kills his *own* people; their history is proof of this. An American President would never think of killing his *own* people.

Saddam's crimes are most foul because he has tortured his *own* people; he has killed his *own* people; he has gassed his *own* people.

He has violated the edict of nature. His actions are so terribly *un*-American.

Saddam's unnatural crimes trouble us, however, not because we feel empathy for his victims. His crimes *predict* trouble for us. If he can kill his *own* kind how much more willingly would he kill *us*? In Scot McClellan's version: "any person that would gas his own people is a threat to the world (read the United States)."

Of course, Saddam might plead innocence to this charge. "You've got it all wrong about the people I kill. The Kurds I killed are not my *own* people. They are not even Arabs and, worse, they wanted to break up Iraq and create their own independent Kurdistan. What would you do to your Blacks, Amerindians, Hispanics or Asians, if they took up arms to carve out independent states of their own? Were not the Southern whites your own people? But you killed a half million Southerners when they took up arms against you in the 1860s. More recently, you killed your own kind at Waco."

Now, as the United States prepares to try Saddam for torturing, gassing and killing his *own* people, does this absolve *us* of killing the same people because *they* are not our *own*? Is the killing of Iraqis a crime only when the perpetrators are local thugs – once in our pay – and not when *we* take up the killing and execute it more efficiently, on *our* account?

In the colonial era, racism inoculated people against feeling empathy towards those *other* people in the Periphery. Those *other* people were children, barbarians, savages, if not worse. We had to kill them if they could not be useful to us, or if they stood in the way of *our* progress. There wasn't much squeamishness about that. It was good policy.

In the era of the Cold War, we went easy on the language of racism, though not always on its substance. When we sent our men and women to kill hundreds of thousands of Vietnamese and Koreans, we justified this by claiming that we were doing it to protect *our* freedoms. Of course, it was all right to kill others for *our* freedoms.

However, in the new era, the US contracted the killing to thugs in the Periphery. This was a win-win for us. We kept our hands free from bloodstains, so we could smell like roses. At the same time, we could point to colored killers (in our pay), and say, "Look, they are still incapable of civilization." What is more, we could use their savagery as justification for killing colored peoples on our own account.

More recently, the US has gone back to killing on its own account. Starting in the 1980s, taking advantage of their costly foreign debts – which we helped create – we began a general economic warfare against the Periphery, stripping down their economies for takeover by Core capital. In this new war, the colonial governors and viceroys have been replaced by two banks – the World Bank and the IMF – and a trade enforcer, the WTO. Like the famines in British India, this war has produced tens of millions of hidden victims, dead from hunger and disease.

In 1990, the US introduced a new, deadlier form of economic warfare: it placed Iraq under a total siege. This instrument was chosen because we knew that Iraq was vulnerable: it imported much of its food, medicines, medical equipment, machinery and spare parts, nearly all paid for by oil exports. Imposed to end the Iraqi occupation of Kuwait in 1990, the siege was lifted in 2003, some thirteen years later and only *after* the US had occupied Iraq. Altogether, this US-imposed siege had killed more than a million and a half Iraqis, half of them children.

Once again, the US is the world's nerve center of reactionary ideologies. The post-War restraints on the use of deadly force now gone, the United States revels in the use of deadly force. Not that alone, it wants to be *seen* using deadly force. It wants to be feared, even loathed for its magnificent power, raining death from the skies as never before, like no other power before. At manufacturing death, we brook no competition.

Imperialism, militarism and wars create their own rationale. In time, Islamist enemies were created and magnified, with help from the Zionists. Rogue states stepped out of the shadows. The swamps began to spawn terrorists. Weapons of mass destruction proliferated. Sagely Orientalists suddenly awoke to an Arab "democracy deficit." Islam, they declared, is misogynist, anti-modernist and anti-democratic. The civilizing mission was Arabized. Once again, the musty odors of jingoism, militarism, racism and religious bigotry infested the air. Like a godsend, the attacks of September 11, 2001, galvanized America. Imperialism and racism rode into town, cheek by jowl, hand in hand.

The new colonization project has now snagged its chief prize. An Arab Ozymandias brought low. The man who tortured, killed and gassed his *own* people is in American hands. Our civilizing mission displays its trophy. We are repeatedly invited to peep into the oral orifice of this bedraggled Saddam. "Ladie's and gentlemen, we got him."

The images of Saddam the captive, haggard, resigned, defanged, are images of our raw power. Our power to appoint, anoint, finance and arm surrogates in the Periphery: and when they go wrong, our power to wage war against their people; destroy their civilian infrastructure, poison their air, water and soil with uranium; lay siege to their economy; and, finally, to invade and occupy their country. We will go to any lengths to save the people of the Periphery from *our* tyrants.

Come, then, wretched denizens of the Periphery, there is cause to rejoice. Lift your Cokes and offer a toast to the Boy Emperor even as he launches wars to establish a thousand years of Pax Americana. He will bring down all outmoded tyrannies, and root out rogue states, dictatorships and monarchies. He will extirpate all fundamentalists, hunt down all terrorists, track down all drug lords, and scrap all unfriendly WMDs. This will be the great cleansing of all self-created challenges to the Empire. In the end nothing will stand between the Empire and the Periphery, between Capital and Labor, between Thesis and Anti-Thesis.

Rejoice: the Empire is hastening its day of reckoning with history, its tryst with destiny, its speedy descent to memory.

CHAPTER FOURTEEN

A Comic Apology

"There's a lot of people in the world who don't believe that people whose skin color may not be the same as ours can be free and self-govern. I reject that. I reject that strongly. I believe that people who practice the Muslim faith can self-govern. I believe that people whose skins aren't necessarily - are a different color than white can self-govern."

George Bush, April 30, 2004[1]

May 7, 2004

This happens rarely – very rarely. An apology from the President of the United States, not for personal lapses, but for the rare slippage in the workings of America's virtuous, divinely blessed, civilizing mission to the world.

Most Americans truly believe – take this to be self-evident – that the United States is not only the world's greatest country: it is also the last great hope of earth, that Americans have always been willing, more than any other Western power, to take on the White Man's burden, to bring life, liberty and happiness to the rest of mankind.

[1] George Will, "Time for Bush to See The Realities of Iraq," *Washington Post*, May 4, 2004.

This is a testament to the power of American media: that it can claim to be the world's freest media and yet control – like no other 'free' media – what an overwhelming majority of Americans believe about their country. And what they believe is America the free, pure and virtuous.

Day after day, the mandarins and media in this country work tirelessly, cleverly, to project an image of an America that protects freedoms at home and abroad; an America that has time and again shed its blood to rid foreign lands of murderous tyrannies; an America that cares, that responds with alacrity to famines and calamities abroad; an America that contributes men, money and ideas to bring prosperity to the backward races; an America that has selflessly served as an honest broker in the dispute between Israelis and Palestinians.

As a result, year after year, most Americans are kept in the dark, unaware of the *actual*, the *real* America – the only kind seen by much of the rest of the world. This is the America that daily employs its might to mangle the lives of hundreds of millions, that pushes a globalization that devastates the economies of the Third World, that instructs and arms foreign tyrannies to terrorize their own people, that aids and abets an Israeli machine determined to extirpate the Palestinians. This America acts in the name of freedom, in any way that it sees fit and necessary, to keep the world safe for American capital. However, this dark side of America is nearly completely, nearly always, whitewashed by the myth-making powers of America's elites.

Occasionally, this myth-making machine will let slip a few snapshots of the real, the actual America. In fact, such slippages are functional; they serve to validate the trust of the duped and faithful in our 'free' media. Generally, these revelations appear long after the fact. They are also quickly explained away. Americans are told that these slippages are justified by the end they serve: the triumph of higher American values. When they cannot be explained away, they are described as but natural lapses, the human failings of a few. These lapses remind the faithful to be thankful that the system works well nearly all the time. No apology is tendered. None is demanded.

Yet the matter of the torture of Iraqi prisoners has quickly produced a storm of indignation from the mandarins and the media. It has led to calls for investigations, demands for the resignation of the Secretary of Defense, two television appearances by the President before Arab audiences, and, incredibly, even a Presidential apology, albeit a feeble apology. In the words of Scott McClellan, the White House Press Secretary, "The President is sorry for what occurred and the pain it has caused."

I am assuming that the "pain" in question is the one Americans have inflicted on the Iraqis, the same Iraqis whom we had liberated from one tyranny – only to place them under another. Or is the President talking of America's pain over the actual, the real America, now irrevocably, unforgettably, caught on camera? For the history books. For posterity.

In any case, that's quite decent for starters. Incredibly, the name of a sitting American President has been linked to the subject of Arab pain, a pain that has an acknowledged American provenance. It must be a first, for *any* American President – perhaps, any Western leader. We are speaking of the pain of the "natives" – inferior sand niggers, in this case – the pain of whose miserable lives did not deserve to be anointed by our sympathy. We do not share in the pain of the natives.

Has the President undergone another conversion? If he has, and now, he truly and sincerely feels the pain inflicted by a few Americans on their Iraqi victims, will he follow up by acknowledging the

Iraqis who were killed and maimed to advance the interests of Zionists and Oil Corporations? Will he also set up museums to commemorate the deaths of a million and a half Iraqi civilians killed in a previous American war that targeted their civilian infrastructure and followed it up with death-dealing sanctions? Is it just possible that at last the President will begin to recognize the Palestinians as humans, and atone for the pain that he and his predecessors have inflicted upon them for more than fifty years?

Apart from the faithful, no one believes that the President's apology is sincere. In fact, it appears distinctly comical – comical because it is based on false premises. We are behaving as if the sexual humiliation of Iraqi prisoners is the *first* outrage inflicted by the United States on the Muslims. It is unlikely that the Muslims have forgotten, or will soon forget, the hundred lacerations inflicted upon them by America's conjugal embrace of the Israeli Occupation, by its support for corrupt monarchies and dictatorships in the Islamicate world, by the genocidal first Gulf War, by the strangulating sanctions against Iraq that took the lives of three-quarters of a million Iraqi children, and by the routine demonization of Islam by preachers close to this White House. It is comical when a tormentor inflicts a hundred wounds on his victim and then starts apologizing for stepping on his toes.

The apology is comical because the United States has hitherto acted on the premise that the Arabs only respect a stout stick. This is the advice that the Zionists have regularly dished out to their American pupils. In part, this was the advice on which President Bush launched his invasion of Iraq. Topple Saddam, the Arab strongman, and all the Arabs will instantly acknowledge US-Israeli hegemony as the greatest gift to them since the appearance of Islam. So, isn't it a bit comical so soon after the Iraqi invasion to come apologizing to the Arabs? Actually, it is worse than comical. It has to be stupid. It will surely be read by many Muslims – not least, those who are in the Islamist resistance – as a sign of weakness, an admission that America's belligerent approach isn't paying off, that the world's only super power is afraid of Arab outrage.

The President's apology is also targeted at domestic audiences. The pictures of American liberators sexually torturing Iraqis do not make the best commercials for America's high civilizing mission. They might just undermine America's faith in its civilizing mission, the principal ideological prop for its formidable military machine. Some quick action was necessary. Americans were assured that the cases of torture were local, not systemic, and their perpetrators are being punished. There was nothing to worry. America's civilizing mission could not be derailed by the actions of a few rogue elements. America must continue to march forward through the jungles, swamps and deserts of the Third World, bringing freedom, hope and prosperity to the inferior breeds who cannot yet manage their own affairs. The civilizing mission is the sacred trust of the White Man.

Still, we must ask, if there isn't an element of panic in the White House response to the scandal of Iraqi prison torture. The whole administration is apologizing, and doing so repeatedly, with little urging from the cretins who pass for Arab leaders. Unexceptionally, however, the apologies are not for torture, but the abuse or humiliation of Iraqis. Still, the sight of the United States – mighty, swaggering, self-congratulatory, unilateralist – apologizing, somehow, makes an eerie sight. Does this suggest that after all the damned lies to cover for the war, after all the blustering as these lies were exposed, this Administration is finally losing its nerve, losing its cool? Could it be that they too know better than what they put out? Could it be that they too fear that the game they started in Iraq – at the cost of American and Iraqi lives – is over?

PART THREE

Palestine and Israel

CHAPTER FIFTEEN

A Colonizing Project Built on Lies

"*We should there form a portion of a rampart of Europe against Asia, an outpost of civilization as opposed to barbarism. We should as a neutral State remain in contact with all Europe, which would have to guarantee our existence.*"

Theodore Herzl (1896)[1]

"*To make Palestine as Jewish as England is English.*"

Chaim Weizman (1919)[2]

"*We Jews have nothing in common with what is denoted 'the East' and we thank God for it.*"

Ze'ev Jabotinsky[3]

April 18, 2002

It is not an easy life when it must be lived, defended, justified everyday, every hour, before the world, before the bar of one's own conscience, with lies, cover-ups, deceptions and sophistry.

This has been the particular burden of Zionists as they conceived their plan for creating a Jewish colonial-settler state in Palestine; as

---

1 Theodore Herzl, *The Jewish State* (1896):http://www.geocities.com/Vienna/6640/zion/ judenstaadt.html.

2 Avi Shlaim, *The Iron Wall: Israel and the Arab World* (New York: W. W. Norton and Company, 2001): 8

3 Shlaim (2001): 12.

they went about executing this plan on the backs of imperialists powers with wars, massacres and ethnic cleansing; as they have continued to dispossess the Palestinians of the last fragments of their rights and legacy whose Canaanite roots are more ancient than Isaiah, Ezekiel, David and Moses.

In the colonial epoch, when Europeans were the 'master race' – and from that exalted position, enslaved and 'improved' the lesser breeds of Asia and Africa – the Zionists had an easy time with their narrative of lies. They wanted to possess Palestine so that they could create a state that would belong exclusively to European Jewry. In order to possess Palestine, they knew that they would have to dispossess the Palestinians.

In that era of racist discourse, this was not a hard sell. It is true that the Jews were not given entry into the club of Europe's master races. Still, they were a biblical people, and it was from their 'chosen seed' that Jesus had sprung. In Europe's hierarchy of races and peoples, the Jews occupied a position well above the Arab inhabitants of Palestine. The Jews were Israelites, children of Jacob, "born of the spirit," while the Arabs were "born of the flesh," Ishmaelites – children of Hagar, the slave woman.[4]

This was the tenor of the Zionist sales pitch. The Jews are a biblical people, an ancient people, the original and only inhabitants of Palestine, who had preserved their traditions and (implausibly) their racial purity through more than two thousand years of co-habitation and co-mingling in Europe. They are a people without a land, living in exile from the land promised to them by the God of the Jews and Christians. They must now end this exile by returning to Palestine, a land once flowing with milk and honey, but which had declined since their departure into a wilderness, a desert now inhabited by wild Bedouin tribes, nondescript aborigines of no account.

---

[4] Galatians, 4: 28-30.

All this was cleverly captured in the deceptive slogan, first coined by Israel Zangwill in 1897, "A land without a people for a people without a land."[5] This became a leading slogan of the Zionist movement. Unlike other colonialists, who justified their conquests with their pieties about improving the natives, the Zionist settlers would improve the land, since there were no people in Palestine to be improved. After the fact, Israel would justify itself with the claim that it had made the deserts bloom. Those magical blossoms sprouted in lands which only recently had supported Palestinian life – Palestinian homes and villages.

When it was pointed out that Palestine was not empty, that it had close to a million inhabitants, the Zionists pressed two claims, one mythical and another secular. The land was theirs because Yahweh had promised it to them. Since Yahweh, later, also turned out to be the God of the Christians, this argument carried a lot of weight with Christians, who were unhappy about Turkish control over Biblical lands. In the words of Henry Cabot Lodge, a senator from Massachusetts during the 1920s, Turkish control over the holy lands was "one of the great blots on the face of civilization, which ought to be erased."[6]

A secular version of this narrative was also available. The Jews had a historical right to Palestine because they had once lived there; the adjective "historical" carries nearly the same weight for the secular that "divine" does for the faithful. The logic was quaint. No one would ever dream of pressing this claim in a court of law. Who has the greater individual or national claim, under any system of laws, to a land: those who *had* ruled it for a short time, and that too more than two thousand years ago; or those who hold it now and

---

[5] Norman Finkelstein, *Image and Reality of the Israel-Palestine Conflict* (New York: Verso, 1995): 95.

[6] Kathleen Christison, *Perceptions of Palestine* (Berkeley, CA: University of California, 1999): 37.

have held it continuously for thousands of years. But logic did not matter. In this case, those pressing the claims had an affinity with the Europeans, and the opposite party was a barbarous, savage race. Of course, no one asked if those who wanted to 'return' were in fact the descendants of those who had left.

With these weighty arguments, not to mention their financial and political assets, the Zionists handily won the support of the two leading imperialist powers. In 1917 Britain pledged to create a national home for the Jews in Palestine; the US Congress followed suit in 1922. After this, the Palestinians did not have a chance. The Zionist project could only have failed if it did not find takers among the Jews. It appeared at first that the Palestinians were in luck. Most Jewish emigrants from Europe preferred greener pastures in the Americas to the first Zionist settlements in Palestine.

Quaintly, Hitler changed all that. Once the Nazis began their persecution of Jews in the mid-1930s, Jewish emigration to Palestine, which had been a trickle before, turned into a flood. When the Palestinians resisted the colonization of their country, they were brutally suppressed by British and Jewish forces. In 1948, the United Nations, under pressure from the United States, approved a plan to partition Palestine between Jews and Palestinians. It gave 55 percent of historic Palestine to Israel, including most of the coastline and the best agricultural lands, though Jews made up only 31 percent of the population and owned less than 7 percent of the land.

This led to war and, predictably, a victory for the Zionists. The Palestinians had already been crushed by the British during the uprising of 1935-39, while the Arab armies that opposed the creation of Israel were poorly trained, poorly led, outnumbered – yes, they were outnumbered – and without a joint command. Israel won the war handily, acquiring 78 percent of historic Palestine, and drove out 800,000 Palestinians from the areas they controlled. In this first

Israeli-Arab war, the Zionists had nearly achieved their goal. In June 1967, all of Palestine passed under Jewish control.

Almost immediately, the Zionist ideologues began inverting the truth about Israel. A racist, colonial settler-state that was established on the backs of imperial powers, and whose founding was premised on the dispossession of Palestinians, was now cast as a newly independent country, in the same class as India and Indonesia, which had won their independence from colonial occupation. The Zionist struggle was even more heroic because, unlike India and Indonesia, they also had to fight off fanatical Arab neighbors unwilling to accept the existence of Israel.

The chief moral asset of the Zionists in their makeover of Israel was the Holocaust. This had created a vast fund of sympathy for the Jews, sympathy born of guilt. The Zionists conserved this sympathy capital through endless commemoration – in movies, media and museums. Better yet, they augmented the Holocaust capital by arguing that Jews had suffered horrors that were unique in history. Never before had a people been targeted for total extermination; never before had they faced death through incineration. Fortified with the shield of Holocaust capital, and armed with the sword of uniqueness, the Zionists elevated themselves to the status of the super victims of history.

This Holocaust capital placed Israel beyond critique. First, Israel was equated with Jews. Second, Jews were equated with the survivors of the Holocaust. Once these equations were established, Israel became the object of all the natural sympathy that belonged to the Holocaust survivors. As the haven, the last refuge for the world's super victims, Israel was now above reproach. It followed that anyone who dared to call Israel to account could only be an anti-Semite. This was a powerful tactic.

Among other things, this meant that there could be no Palestinian victims. It was logically impossible for a Palestinian to be a victim of Israelis. The Israelis, as survivors of the Holocaust, were super victims. Given this, how could the Israelis victimize anyone? All the talk of Palestinian suffering must be slander, the product of Arab anti-Semitism, which they had borrowed from the Nazis. In the court of Western opinion, the Palestinians did not have a prayer.

Worse, Israeli victimhood nullified Palestinians rights. The rights of the Palestinians – to their land, their freedom and dignity – counted for nothing if they collided with the infinitely superior claims of the Israeli super victims. Indeed, any Palestinian action in defense of their rights – if pressed against Israel – automatically earned the charge of immorality. Thus, Zionists charged that Palestinians, by opposing unrestricted immigration of Jews in the 1930s, had sent Jews to Nazi death camps. Under this logic, the very existence of the Palestinians was immoral.

Israel's victimhood could also justify violence against the Palestinians. The Israelis had earned the right to inflict any violence on the Palestinians that did not exceed their own suffering at the hands of the Nazis. As the world's super victims, there was no risk that their own violence would ever cross the limit where it would become unacceptable. The Israelis would remain blameless as long as they were not transporting Palestinians to gas chambers. Among others, Chaim Weizmann, the first president of Israel, employed this logic when protesting the West's muted concerns over the condition of Palestinian refugees. The problem of Palestinian refugees, he argued, was nothing compared to the murder of six million Jews.

It was easy stripping the Palestinians of their most basic rights – to their homes, lands, villages, towns, heritage and history. The Israelis demolished these rights with propaganda masquerading as history. The Palestinians had forfeited these rights because they had fled their homes voluntarily, following orders from Arab radio stations; they were not fleeing from Jewish terror. This concoction entered history books in Israel and the United States. No one asked for the evidence; no one asked if this made sense. No one asked if the Zionists had not planned this exodus all along. After all, how could a Jewish state *in* Palestine exist with all the Palestinians still in place?

The Zionist ideologues went about demonizing the Arabs too. They argued that the Arabs rejected the 1948 partition of Palestine because of a primeval Arab hatred for Jews, hatred that is akin to European anti-Semitism. The Arabs were excoriated for doing what any people faced with destruction would have done – fight against those who sought their destruction. Implicitly, the Zionists argued that the Arabs, or any race of inferior worth, did not possess a right to defend themselves against destruction by a superior people, such as the European Zionists.

In a similar vein, they have argued that Arab refusal to integrate Palestinian "refugees" demonstrated Arab intransigence and, not to forget, perversity. Wars have always created refugees, the Zionists maintained, but they do not linger in refugee camps; they are routinely absorbed by the host countries. If the Palestinians still live in refugee camps – in Jordan, Lebanon, Egypt and Syria – that is because these Arab countries have used them as pawns in their campaign against Israel. The Palestinians too have cooperated in this dastardly game – by refusing to leave the camps.

This is standard Israeli practice: denouncing their victims for not cooperating in their own demise. Israel engaged in large-scale ethnic cleansing of Palestinians because *it had to*; this was a *necessary* consequence of the Zionist plan for a Jewish state in Palestine. Why cannot the Arabs and Palestinians see this? The Palestinians should have gone gently into the good night of national extinction prepared for them by the Zionists; they and their Arab compatriots display nothing but their inveterate anti-Semitism in demanding the right of return. Why should Israel alone have to endure such baseless, boundless hatred?

There was a deeper irony in the Zionist position. The Zionists demanded that the Arab countries should solve the problem of Palestinian refugees. Jordan, Lebanon and Syria hosted them: so they should absorb them. There would be no Zionism if the same logic were applied to the Jews who had lived in Europe for more than two thousand years. Instead, the Zionists argued that the Jewish communities in Italy, Britain, France, Russia and Spain were a distinct people who must have a separate homeland. Worse, that homeland for a European people was not to be founded in Europe, but in Palestine.

A new lie was born when Arafat rejected the scraps offered to the Palestinians at Camp David in July 2000. The lie is that Arafat walked away from "an extremely generous offer," which gave the Palestinians 90 percent of the West Bank and Gaza. Indeed, the offer made at Camp David was very generous to Israel: it gave the Israelis control over the borders of the West Bank and Gaza, their water resources, their air space, and nearly all of old Jerusalem. Israel would keep most of the settlements, together with road links to Israel that Palestinians would need permits to cross. Camp David demanded that the Palestinians formalize a new system of apartheid sponsored and protected by the United States.

Once the second Intifada started and the Palestinians were back in the streets, fighting Israeli armor with stones, the Israeli Occupation Army responded predictably. Within the first week, they had killed more than a hundred Palestinians, many of them children. However, this was no problem for the Israelis. When the world took notice, this was expertly blamed on Palestinian parents. "Look, how much they hate us. Now, they are sacrificing their children to gain some cheap publicity." In no time, the American media, always taking their cue from Israeli officials, were parroting these meretricious charges.

And so the lies, deceptions and sophistry employed to defeat the Palestinians have persisted. Indeed, they have multiplied and metamorphosed to suit the changing circumstances, the changing needs of an anachronistic colonizing project. As soon as Israeli officials announce these lies, they are taken up by a thousand American anchors, reporters and columnists, taken up and circulated verbatim. They rapidly enter into American public discourse, sanctified by op-ed writers, bandied at Congressional hearings, and trumpeted by Presidential hopefuls. Israeli lies become history in America.

Over the past eighty years, the myths created by the Zionist colonizers have killed Arabs, Jews and a few Americans too. They have become venerable like the biblical narratives – of Cain's murder, Ham's curse, Hagar's abandonment – that have supported generations of murderous ideologies. These mythologies, old and new-fangled, will continue to poison the world as long as long as they command our attention, as long as they substitute for history. If we do not oppose these lies here in the United States, they may well end up destroying our dearest hope – of a better world, a humane world, united, giving an equal place to every branch of the human family. We must oppose these myths before they destroy our humanity, child by child, house by house, camp by camp, city by city – as they do today, in Nablus, Tulkaram, Qalqiliya, Ramallah, Bethlehem and Jenin.

CHAPTER SIXTEEN

Academic Boycott of Israel

"Allah forbiddeth you not those who warred not against you on account of religion and drove you not out from your homes, that ye should show them kindness and deal justly with them. Lo! Allah loveth the just dealers."

Qur'ān: 60: 8

July 21, 2002

In early April 2002, moved by the massacres in Jenin and the wanton destruction of civilian infrastructure in the West Bank cities by the Israeli Occupation forces, two British academics, Hilary Rose and Steven Rose, circulated a call for an academic boycott of Israel.[1]

This campaign was directed primarily at European academics, and so when it reached me nearly two months later, in the first week of July 2002, there were only six American academics among the signatories. I carefully read the boycott statement, which entailed non-cooperation with "official Israeli institutions, including universities," and decided to sign on to the list. I also forwarded the call to friends on my e-mail list.

[1] The call for this boycott is posted at www.pjpo.org.

Most of my friends chose to ignore my email. I cannot be sure if they were opposed to the boycott in principle, or did not wish to incur the risk of supporting it. Only two responded to my email, and both were more than a bit troubled that I should be supporting such an initiative. One described this campaign as "destructive;" another objected that this was an "attack" on academic freedom. Once my name was on the list of signatories, I also received two pieces of hate mail.

Soon, Leonid Ryzhik, a mathematics lecturer at the University of Chicago, initiated a counter petition. In an interview published in *The Guardian*, May 27, 2002, he said that the boycott campaign was "immoral, dangerous and misguided, and indirectly encourages the terrorist murderers in their deadly deeds."[2] In addition, this week, in *The Nation*, August 5-12, Martha Nussbaum, an eminent ethical philosopher, wrote that she felt "relaxed" to be in Israel, where she had gone to receive an honorary degree from the University of Haifa, "determined to affirm the worth of scholarly *cooperation* in the face of the ugly campaign (emphasis added)."

Having declared my support for the academic boycott of Israel, I believe I must now explain why I do not view this campaign as "destructive," "ugly" or supportive of "terrorist murderers." On the contrary, I see this as a moral gesture, part of a growing campaign by international civil society to use its moral force to nudge Israelis, to awaken them to the ugly and destructive reality of their Occupation, which has now lasted for more than thirty-five years and shows no sign of ending any time soon. At last, the cumulative weight of Palestinian suffering has begun to break through the crust of Israeli protestations of innocence. Although tardy, world conscience is now preparing to engage Israeli intransigence.

---

[2] Leonid Ryzhik's campaign against the academic boycott of Israel call is posted at www.petitiononline.com/ noboyctt/petition.html.

Increasingly, the world outside the United States understands that Israel is not a normal country. The Zionist movement sought to establish an exclusively Jewish state in Palestine, a land inhabited almost entirely by Palestinian Arabs in 1900 and for many centuries before that. Since no people yet have been known to commit collective suicide, or followed the Nazarene precept of turning the other cheek to its tormentor, the Zionists would have to achieve their objective through old-fashioned means: conquest *and* ethnic cleansing. This is how Israel emerged in 1948, through conquest and ethnic cleansing of 800,000 Palestinians.

Yet this was not enough. Although Israel now sat on 78 percent of historic Palestine, this was still short of Zionist goals. In 1967, during its pre-emptive war against Egypt, Syria and Jordan, Israel corrected this shortfall. It occupied the West Bank and Gaza. In addition, the Israelis pushed another 300,000 Palestinians across the Jordan River.

Although the Security Council promptly called upon Israel to withdraw from the territories it had occupied in 1967, this resolution had no teeth. After routing three Arab armies, two from the leading nationalist Arab states, Israel succeeded in deepening its special relationship with the United States; this promptly led to a doubling in US military and economic assistance to Israel. Seen from the Arab world, Israel and the United States now became two faces of the same reality. Jointly, and with increasing success, they sought to destroy Arab nationalist aspirations.

As a result, thirty-five years later, Israel still occupies the West Bank and Gaza. In reality, this 'Occupation' is merely a fiction, a farcical cover under which Israel buys time, which it uses to insert armed Israeli settlers, to increase Israeli control and ownership of Palestinian lands, to push the Palestinians into ever shrinking enclaves, to escalate the violence against Palestinian resistance, and to deepen the misery of Palestinian lives, all in pursuit of a policy of slow ethnic cleansing. At the same time, Israelis prepare for a final round of ethnic cleansing.

The logic of the Occupation is transparent to all but the purblind. If Palestinian demography prevents annexation, and ethnic cleansing is not feasible at present, the creation of Bantustans in the West Bank offers the next best solution. If 1.3 million Palestinians can be contained in Gaza, with an area of 360 square kilometers, the creation of similar enclaves in the West Bank could free up 90 percent of it for Jewish settlements. It is time to give up the fiction of the Occupation, and describe this oppressive regime by its proper name. This is a new Apartheid: one country with two unequal peoples, Jews and Palestinians, the colonizers and the colonized.

I have two objectives in rehearsing the narrative of Palestinian dispossession. First, the Zionists have repeatedly denied and massively falsified this narrative. Therefore, we must affirm it, simply and forcefully, again and again, in the expectation that world conscience will bear witness to the Zionist project of wiping out the Arab presence from Palestine to make room for Jewish settlers.

Once we affirm this narrative; once we recognize that the creation of Israel was based on the destruction of Palestinians; once we admit that the dispossession of Palestinians was implemented through wars, ethnic cleansing, massacres, villages destroyed, cities besieged, homes demolished, children maimed and killed, prisoners tortured, ambulances bombed, journalists targeted, municipal records destroyed and trees uprooted; once we recognize all this destructiveness – already accomplished, and more of it unfolding everyday – the accusations about the "destructiveness" or "ugliness" of an academic boycott of Israel will be seen for what they are – ludicrous and, indeed, unconscionable.

Mr. Leonid Ryzhik argues that the academic boycott "indirectly encourages the [Palestinian] terrorist murderers in their deadly deeds." Does he mean to say that this boycott "indirectly encourages" the Palestinian resistance? Is the boycott troubling because it seeks to question, delay and obstruct the extension of the Zionist project to the West Bank and Gaza? We must affirm in the face of such posturing that resistance is an inalienable right of the Palestinians, as it was of all colonized peoples who have faced dispossession. Of necessity, colonial dispossession is implemented by force, by massive force; it follows, that if the victim *so* chooses, resistance to dispossession can also employ violent means.

The question is not, why do the Palestinians resist, or why do they resist by violent means? There is a different question before world conscience. Why have we for fifty years abandoned the Palestinians to fight their battles alone, beleaguered by a colonizer whom they cannot fight alone? Why have we remained passive while the Palestinians were battered, exiled from their lands, herded into villages and towns that have been turned into concentration camps, exposed to the mercy of a colonizer who freely draws upon the finances, political support and military arsenal of the world's greatest power? In despair, marginalized, pauperized, and facing extinction as a people, if the Palestinians now use the only defense they have – to weaponize their death – who is to blame?

Finally, as Western conscience engages the Palestinian question, we can hope that this will mitigate the deep despair of Palestinians. When they learn that academic communities in Britain, France, Germany, Canada and the United States, hitherto indifferent to their tragic plight, are calling on Israel to end their Apartheid, the Palestinians may rethink their tactics. When they can see that Western audiences too are beginning to see the justice of their cause, the Palestinians may choose to renounce their acts of desperation. The academic boycott of Israel leverages moral suasion to reduce the violence of the colonizer as well as the colonized.

There are people who are shouting "Foul" at the academic boycott on the plea that this curtails the academic freedom of Israelis. I will readily admit that it does; this boycott can only work by shrinking some of the international avenues available to Israeli scientists for pursuing their work. Still, this curtailment is temporary; it will end the instant Israel ends the Occupation. It is also of limited scope. It only seeks to limit some of the advantages Israeli scientists derive from their interactions with the global scientific community. It does not threaten any fundamental academic freedoms.

In addition, we must look upon this curtailment of academic freedom in a larger context. Although academic freedom is an important value, one that all civilized societies should cherish, it is not an absolute value; there are other values that we cherish, other values that are more important, more fundamental than the right to academic freedom. I believe it is reasonable and moral to impose temporary and partial limits on the academic freedom of a *few* Israelis if this can help to restore the fundamental rights of millions of Palestinians – to life, to property, to ancestral lands, to sovereign control over their destiny, and to equal treatment under the law. We can deny this only if we confess to a disproportion in the value we accord to Israeli and Palestinian rights.

I refuse to be intimated by the cant about the 'sanctity' of academia, about mixing politics and science. More than ever before, universities help to reproduce the power structures of their societies; they are a potent source of ideologies of imperialism, race and class exploitation. Israeli universities are no exception. Through their links with the military, the political parties, the media and the economy, they have helped to construct, sustain and justify Israeli Apartheid. I might have hesitated in adding my name to the boycott if I knew that

Israeli academics had taken the lead in organizing rallies, staging sit-ins, passing resolutions protesting the Occupation, refusing military service in the Occupied territories, or working on projects that reinforced the Occupation. On the contrary, nearly all of Israeli academia has shown that it is a party to the Occupation.

Of course, one might argue that this boycott is wasted effort; it can have no appreciable impact on Israeli society and policies. This is a question about the efficacy of the boycott. It is well known that Israeli scientists cherish the cooperation of the world's scientific community as well as access to international funding. We can expect, therefore, that if the boycott spreads, this can begin to reduce the effectiveness of Israeli scientists. Perhaps more important, Israelis will find it harder to ignore the message that the boycott sends to them: that Israeli violations of Palestinian rights are repugnant and will not be allowed to stand.

The academic boycott is one of the few handles that international civil society can use to bring pressure against Israeli Apartheid. Because of the power of the pro-Israeli lobbies in the United States, Israel continues to violate Palestinian rights with impunity. If any other country had been guilty of similar violations – nay, even half those violations – it would have invited economic sanctions, and even military intervention from the United Nations.

The capitulation of the United States to the pro-Israeli lobby has serious consequences for Palestinians and the future of world peace. It has meant that Israel can wage war against a civilian population – using jets, rockets, tanks, armored vehicles, explosives and bulldozers – with impunity. Abandoned, isolated, beleaguered and unarmed, a few Palestinian men and women have responded to this massive force by weaponizing their own death, provoking still greater violence from the Israeli military machine. Paradoxically, by the deaths they inflict and their own, the Palestinian 'suicide bombers' have forced world conscience to acknowledge that if they act beyond the pale of reason it is because the Israeli Occupation – so rational, so methodical, so streamlined, so overwhelming in its efficiency – leaves them with few tools with which to resist but the sacrifice of their own lives. The academic boycott is one small step that a slowly detribalizing world has now taken to stop the daily affront to our common humanity that is perpetrated in the West Bank and Gaza. This symbolic act should be endorsed, even applauded, by all men and women who have already risen above tribalism.

CHAPTER SEVENTEEN

Crossing the Line

"O ye who believe! Endure, outdo all others in endurance, be ready, and observe your duty to Allah, in order that ye may succeed."

Qur'ān: 3: 200

"This book sounds an alarm: Israel, through the deep and pervasive power of its lobby, threatens deeply-cherished American values—especially free speech, academic freedom and our commitment to human rights."

Paul Findley (1985)[1]

September 16, 2002

In 1982, when Paul Findley went down in his re-election bid after serving in the Congress for twenty-two years, the principal pro-Israeli lobby in Washington took credit for his defeat. What was the Congressman's crime? He had crossed a line drawn by the Israeli lobby in the United States: he had violated the Israeli ban on meeting Arafat.

---

[1] Paul Findley, *They Dare to Speak Out* (Westport, CT.: Lawrence Hill and Co., 1985): v.

This past week I too had a little taste of the same medicine. No, I am not a public figure, nor had I met with Arafat or any other Palestinian degraded to "terrorist" ranks by Israel's lexical offensive. I am only a professor, an obscure peddler of dissent, who, once tenure was secured, had been left reasonably well alone by school administrators, colleagues, and assorted self-appointed censors. How then did I get into trouble?

Over the past year, I began to cross that thin line, which I should have known one crosses only at some peril. I began to talk and write about Israel. This would not have been remarkable if I had been reading from the script; but I was not. Instead, I began to call a spade a spade. In other words, I was stepping over the line.

Although invisible, this line is like a charged electrical cable. I first stepped on this cable when I spoke on the attacks of 9-11 at Northeastern University in October 2001. I had planned on providing a historical backdrop to the attacks on the Twin Towers, drawing attention to the record of French, British and American interventions in the region. My principal concern was that some Americans, so soon after September 11, might greet such an attempt with hostility. To my pleasant surprise, I was wrong. At the end of the seminar, several students and faculty stepped forward to thank me for speaking out.

However, the matter did not end there. A few hours after the talk, the Chair of Economics informed me that a professor (not from my own department) had emailed to complain that I had "deviated" from the announced theme of the seminar. Later, the same day, as I was walking across the campus, a professor, one I had never met before, accosted me. He told me that he was at my talk, and proceeded to accuse me of "hate speech." I could think of one passing reference to the history of Israel – its colonial-settler character – which had nettled this professor who will not allow the mythology of Israel to be challenged in a rational discourse.

Disoriented by the attacks on the Twin Towers, many Americans felt that the 9-11 had "changed everything." I shared in America's grief at the wanton loss of human lives, the first in their recent history. Although I had known this grief before, many times before, September 11 was changing me too. I was concerned over the curtailment of civil liberties in the United States, the growing attacks on Islam, and the triumph of lobbies who wanted the United States to wage endless wars against the rest of the world. Stepping out of my academic shell, I felt it was time to speak to some real issues.

Among other things, in early April I signed a petition that called for the academic boycott of Israel. In addition, I forwarded the petition to a few colleagues at Northeastern University. When one of them objected to this boycott, and declared that it is "destructive," I had to explain why I thought this campaign was morally justified. I wrote an essay, "An Academic Boycott of Israel," which was first published in *Counterpunch.Org* on July 31, 2002; it has since appeared on many more websites, newspapers and discussion groups. This produced both angry and supportive emails; only one threatened violence. Overall, I was pleased at the response.

There was worse to come. On September 3, 2002, the *Jerusalem Post* carried a report on my essay under the heading, "US Prof Justifies Palestinian Terror Attacks." The *Post* report did not mention the title of my essay or give any hint of its substance. The next morning I received several angry emails. Some of these were copied to the Chair of Economics and other administrators at Northeastern University. Over the next two days, I received calls from *The Jewish Advocate*, *Boston Herald*, *Bloomberg News* and *The O'Reilly Factor*. Although flattered by the attention, I declined the invitation to meet the honorable Mr. Bill O'Reilly.

On September 5, taking the cue from the *Post*, the *Herald* published another malicious and sensational report on my essay. It was headlined, "Prof Shocks Northeastern with Defense of Suicide Bombers." It claimed that my article "sent shock-waves through the Fenway campus yesterday," but quoted only one Professor at Northeastern. The *Herald* report too did not refer to the title or substance of my essay, justifiably raising suspicions about the reporter's motive. Although I had sent a timely response to their email, the *Herald* reporter claimed that he could not contact me by phone or email.

It is curious how these reports had inverted the objective of my essay. My essay made a case for an academic boycott, a quintessentially non-violent act, as an alternative to the recent Palestinian acts of desperation. By showing greater solicitude for the Palestinians' desperate plight, I argued, international civil society could give hope to this beleaguered people, and persuade them to act with greater patience in the face of Israel's brutal military Occupation. The *Post* and *Herald* had twisted a moral case for non-violent action into justification for terror.

It would appear that I had crossed the 'line' in advocating an academic boycott of Israel, and I had to be punished. To quote Taha Abdul-Basser (*Boston Herald*, September 9), what the *Post* and *Herald* "actually find distasteful is the thought that intelligent, well-spoken people of conscience should call for a moral stand against the oppressive and unjust behavior of Israel." At least in the United States, the Israeli narrative has nearly monopolized public discourse on policies towards the Middle East. This narrative speaks only of Jewish claims to Palestine, and presents Israel as a victim of Arab hatred of all things Western, a beleaguered outpost of Western civilization in an ocean of Arab barbarism. My essay was unacceptable because it questions this narrative.

The attacks against me perhaps are not over yet. As I was finishing this essay on the night of September 8, I learned that I had been 'spoofed' – an addition to my lexicon. Someone had stolen my identity and sent out e-mails, containing malicious anti-Semitic diatribe, to administrators and colleagues at Northeastern. The spoof was quite crude, making it hard for anyone who knew me to believe that it could have originated from me. Or, perhaps, I am being naïve.

In the days following the September 11 attacks, President Bush had advanced a vision of the world framed in Manichean terms. Either you are with us, or you are against us. The Arabs are evildoers. We have always been good to them; they attack us only because they envy our freedom and our prosperity. Dissenting with President Bush was blasphemous; it gave comfort to terrorists. This is the new-fangled theology of America's war against terrorism, whose ramifications are being worked out feverishly every day by hawks of every stripe.

America's "war against terrorism" is legitimizing state terror the world over. Israel, Russia, China, India and many lesser powers have appropriated this new theology to suppress the legitimate resistance of various oppressed peoples as terrorist activities. In addition, America's hawkish lobbies are using the new theology to stifle discourse by smearing their opponents with the brush of terrorism. The *Post* and *Herald* have employed this tactic against me.

If we allow these attacks on free speech to stand, if we allow the corporate media, the right-wing zealots and pro-Israeli lobby to regulate our thoughts, we may soon witness the narrowing of all discourse to the parroting of official lies, we will be rallying behind illegal wars, and applauding the curtailment of our own liberties. We will only be free to mouth slogans. "Down with our enemies! Down with terrorism! Down with Arabs! Down with Islam!"

CHAPTER EIGHTEEN

Israelization of the United States

"And even so do We try some of them by others, that they say: Are these they whom Allah favoreth among us?"

Qur'ān: 6: 53

April 5, 2003

The images of the American armada plowing through the deserts of Iraq, bombing military and civilian targets, laying siege to Iraqi cities, targeting Iraqi leaders, shooting civilians, blinded by sandstorms, stalled, ambushed, shocked by the Iraqi resistance, facing suicide attacks, suggests an eerie but inescapable comparison. Is this America's West Bank? Is this the Israelization of the United States – heading to its logical conclusion?

Most Americans have been taught by their captive media to interpret what happens *today* in the Middle East in terms of what happened *yesterday*. The clock of history in this region always starts with the most recent "suicide" attack mounted by Palestinians against "peaceful," "innocent" Israeli "civilians." If, somehow, these Americans could be persuaded to take the long view, they might begin to understand that the war against Iraq is perhaps the culmination of a process that had been long in the making: the Israelization of the United States.

The founding fathers of Zionism understood clearly that *their* colonial project had no chance of succeeding without the patronage of a great power. The Zionists tried but failed to persuade the Ottoman Caliph to open up Palestine to Jewish colonization; he declined their financial inducements. Then, the British found themselves in a tight spot in the midst of World War I. They sought Jewish help in accelerating US entry into the war. In return for their help, the Zionists got the vital support they had sought since 1897. In the infamous Balfour Declaration of November 1917, the British promised "to use their best endeavor" (what charming language) to facilitate the creation of a "national home for the Jewish people" in Palestine.

The British occupied Palestine in December 1917 and immediately opened it up to Jewish immigration. At the end of the war, according to the terms of a secret agreement, the British and French vivisected the Arab territories of the Ottoman Empire to splinter Arab unity. Syria was carved up four ways: Lebanon, to create a Maronite-dominated state; Jordan, to reward one of the sons of the collaborating Sharif Hussein of Mecca; a French-controlled Syria; and the British mandate of Palestine, the future Israel. Soon, the Jews of Europe came pouring into British-occupied Palestine, setting up a parallel government with their own military.

The die was cast for the Palestinians. They were no match for the combined Zionist and British forces; and there was no help from weak Arab 'states' hamstrung by imperialist control. Still the Palestinians fought to save their homeland. When the British halted Jewish immigration into Palestine in 1939, the Zionists mounted a terrorist campaign. The British lost nerve and passed the buck to the United Nations or, effectively, to the United States, which now dominated that august body. Motivated in part by anti-Semitism and still strong Christian sentiments, but also swayed by a determined Jewish campaign, the United States pushed a partition plan that strongly favored the Jews. The Palestinians rejected the partition plan. They and other Arabs mounted a feeble resistance, but were routed by the Zionists. In 1948, the Israelis expelled 800,000 Palestinians from their homes (in what became Israel) and never allowed them to return.

It should be understood that the creation of Israel did not – at least in the early years – advance America's strategic interests. At the time, the United States and Britain exercised firm – and very profitable – control over the oil resources of the Gulf through a clutch of weak and pliant monarchies. The emergence of radical governments in Egypt in 1952, and, later, Syria, only deepened the dependence of the oil-rich Arab monarchies on Western powers. When the Iranian nationalists sought to nationalize their oil in 1952, the Americans and British organized a coup, and reinstated the deposed King. In other words, the British and Americans were firmly in control of the region – without any help from Israel. A "special relationship" with the Israeli interloper could only undermine this control by inflaming Arab nationalist sentiments.

The record of American assistance to Israel shows that the special relationship did not develop until the late 1960s. US aid flows to Israel remained well below $100 million annually until 1965, and, more importantly, very little of this was for military hardware. The aid flows doubled in 1966, increased six fold in 1971, and five fold again in 1974 when it rose to $2.6 billion, going up to $5 billion in more recent years.[1] Further, this aid was disbursed mostly in the form of grants, and nearly all of it was spent on military hardware. Indeed, these terms indicate a very "special relationship," not available to any other country.

Most commentators, especially those on the left, attribute the emergence of this special relationship to Israel's stunning 1967

---

[1] "U.S. Assistance to Israel," Jewish Virtual Library: http://www.us-israel.org/jsource/US-Israel/U.S._Assistance_to_Israel1.html (2003).

victory over Egypt, Syria and Jordan. They argue that this victory convinced the US that Israel could serve as a vital ally and a counterpoise to Arab nationalism and Soviet ambitions in the region. But this explanation is both one-sided and simplistic. It completely ignores the part Israel played in initiating this relationship, deepening it and making it irreversible.

If the special relationship was the product of an Israeli victory over Arabs, the US should have embraced Israel as a vital ally after its first victory over Arab armies in 1948 or after 1956 when it seized the entire Sinai in a lightning strike. Why did US have to wait until 1967 *after* Israel had humiliated the leading nationalist states and Soviet allies in the region? Arguably, the Arab *defeat* should have reduced Israel's usefulness to the US. In addition, the doubling of American aid flows to Israel in 1966 as well as the cover-up of the 1967 Israeli attack on the USS Liberty – a reconnaissance ship – off the Sinai coast, indicate that a special relationship had been developing well before the 1967 war.

If America's special relationship with Israel was slow to develop, in large part, this was because *Israel* was doing quite well without it. At least in the 1950s, the British were still the paramount power in the Persian Gulf, a position it would yield only slowly to the United States. In addition, Israel entered into a very fruitful military relationship with France, who supplied not only heavy arms and combat aircraft but collaborated on its nuclear weapons program. Israel was quite confident of its military superiority over its Arab adversaries even in these early years. Apparently, the British and the French too knew about this, since they persuaded Israel to invade Sinai in 1956 as part of their campaign to regain control of the Suez Canal. This confidence was well-placed. Within a few days, Israel had taken the Sinai from the Egyptians.

If the war of 1967 produced stunning Israeli victories, it also drove Israel to look for a new partner. First, since it had started the war against French advice, President De Gaulle suspended all arms shipments to Israel. In order to make good the loss, Israel turned to the US, which had the added advantage of being the world leader in military technology. At the same time, Egypt and Syria would seek to rebuild their decimated military by pursuing an even closer relationship with Soviet Union. Given the logic of the Cold War, this persuaded the US to develop Israel as a counterweight against the growing Soviet influence in the region. The conditions were now ripe for the growth of a special relationship between Israel and the US.

The Israeli decision to realign itself with the US was pregnant with consequences. Israel would have to persuade Americans that their vital interests in the region – protecting their oil supplies, rolling back Arab nationalism, and containing Soviet influence – could be best served by building up Israel, militarily and economically, as the regional hegemon. This would not be an easy task since American support for Israel was certain to alienate the Arab world. And Americans knew this.

The Israelis undertook this task with seriousness. In casting itself as the regional hegemon, Israel was playing a high-risk, high-stakes game that could succeed only if it was supported and financed by the US. Moreover, Israel could not build a new strategy on a special relationship that Americans would be free to reverse. In order to make this an enduring relationship, Israel would bolster it at two levels.

At the grass-roots level, the Israeli lobbies worked to build an emotionally intense American identification with Israel. This was pursued in a variety of ways. Most importantly, American consciousness was saturated with guilt over Jewish suffering. In his book, *The Holocaust Industry*, Norman Finkelstein has shown that the sacralization of the holocaust began only *after* 1967, and how the guilt this produced has been used to silence Israel's critics. Americans now feared that criticism of Israel would be seen as anti-Semitism. As a result, few dared to criticize Israel in public.

Israel was also portrayed as a democracy, constantly under attack from Palestinians and Arabs. Two explanations of Arab hatred of Israel were offered. It was a species of anti-Semitism. Like its older European cousin, Arab anti-Semitism was unprovoked; it had no causes. Alternatively, unable to modernize, the Arabs hated Israel because it was the only country in the region that was both free and prosperous.

At the political level, organized American Jewry amplified its efforts to increase the pro-Israeli bias of American politics. While individual Jews continued to play a distinguished role in liberal and left causes, nearly all the major Jewish organizations now worked feverishly to put pressure on the media, the Congress and the Presidency to offer unconditional support to Israel. In several states, Jewish money, votes and media tilted elections towards the most pro-Israeli candidates. In addition, Jewish organizations worked more effectively to *defeat* candidates who took positions even mildly critical of Israel. This is documented in Paul Findley's book, *They Dare to Speak Out*.

Once Israel's special relationship with the US was in place, it would acquire its own logic of success. This logic worked through several channels. First, as Jewish organizations worked to shape US policies towards Israel, they would improve their tactics, and their initial victories would bring more Jewish support and, in time, more success. This logic even worked to turn temporary reverses to Israel's advantage. People who argue that the US special relationship with Israel was prompted by its victory in 1967 should also note that its near-defeat in 1973 led, the following year, to a more than five-fold increase in the US aid package to Israel to $2.6 billion. Egypt took this message to heart, deciding that it would be futile to challenge this special relationship any further. In 1978, it signed a separate peace with Israel, after the US promised to sweeten the deal with an annual aid package of $2 billion. Its chief rival eliminated, Israeli hegemony over the Middle East was now more secure.

Iran's Islamist revolution in 1979 added new strength to Israel's special relationship with the US. The overthrow of the Iranian monarchy, the second pillar of American hegemony in the Middle East, increased Israel's leverage over US policies. In addition, the accession to power of Islamists raised the bogey of an Islamic threat to the West. The Israeli lobby, especially its Middle East experts, had been making the case for some time that the Islamist movements in the Middle East opposed the US *per se*, and not merely its policies towards Israel. The alarm caused by the Iranian Revolution gave strength to this interpretation.

The end of the Cold War in 1990 stripped the special relationship of its old rationale. Israel would now have to invent a new one to continue to sell itself as a strategic asset. It would now market itself as the barrier, the breakwater, against the rising tide of Islamic fundamentalism. For many years, the chief opposition to the corrupt and repressive regimes in the Arab world, whether dictatorships or monarchies, had taken Islamist forms. Pro-Israeli apologists in the media and academia – mostly Jewish neoconservatives and Middle East experts – argued that the West now faced a new Islamic enemy, global in its reach, who hated the freedoms, secular values and prosperity of the West. Bernard Lewis, the "doyen" of Middle East experts and a passionate Zionist, solemnly intoned in 1993 that this was nothing less than a "clash of civilizations." This was a clever move, but also a necessary one, to convert Israel's conflict with the Arabs into a new Crusade, the war of the West (read the United

States) against Islamdom. It was a clever move also because it had support from Christian fundamentalists, who were now a strong force in the Republican Party.

The new Crusaders worked in tandem with Islamicate extremists in the Al-Qaida camp who also wanted to provoke a war between Islamdom and the US. Every time Osama's men struck at American targets, it was exploited by the pro-Israeli lobby to promote the Clash thesis. When the nineteen hijackers struck on September 11, 2001, they could not have chosen a better time. The man at America's helm was a born-again Christian, backed by right-wing Christians, and with a cabinet that took its advice on foreign policy mostly from neoconservatives with strong Israeli ties. The neoconservative's plan for a new Crusade had been ready long before 9-11. They had the President's ear after 9-11, and the President bought into their plan.

In no time, George Bush had been converted into a new Crusader. He described Ariel Sharon as a "man of peace," after embracing every one of his extremist positions on the Palestinians: reoccupation of the West Bank, repudiation of Oslo, removal of Arafat and dismantling of the Palestinian authority. He laid out his binary doctrine – you are with us or against-us – and prepared for pre-emptive wars against the "axis of evil."

The new Crusade is now underway. The world's only superpower, commanding one-fifth of the world's output, and nearly one-half its military expenditure, has entered Iraq to effect regime-change, to bring 'democracy' to a people it has emasculated with bombs and sanctions for twelve years. In this new Crusade, the United States stands at the head of a numerous "coalition of the coerced," now including forty-five countries. However, America's "strategic asset in the Middle East," Israel, is prominently missing from this long list of coalition partners. That is a trick no magician could replicate. The Israelization of the United States is complete.

CHAPTER NINETEEN

Illuminating Thomas Friedman

"Among the People of the Scripture there is he who, if thou trust him with a weight of treasure, will return it to thee. And among them there is he who, if thou trust him with a piece of gold, will not return it to thee unless thou keep standing over him. That is because they say: We have no duty to the Gentiles."

Qur'ān: 3: 75

June 18, 2003

The publishers, Farrar, Straux & Giroux, maintain a webpage on Thomas Friedman, the foreign affairs columnist for the *New York Times*. The webpage proudly proclaims that Friedman is in a "unique position to interpret the world for American readers. Twice a week, Friedman's commentary provides the most trenchant, pithy, and illuminating perspective in journalism."[1]

I will not contest the claim that Mr. Friedman is in "a *unique position* to interpret the world for American readers (emphases added)." That is plain enough: he writes for the *NYT*, arguably America's most influential newspaper. However, do his commentaries

[1] "Thomas L. Friedman," Farrar, Straus & Giroux (2002-2003): http://www.thomaslfriedman.com/index.htm.

provide "the most trenchant, pithy, and illuminating perspective in journalism"? What do his commentaries "illuminate" – his Middle Eastern subjects or his own biases?

Consider his column, "The Reality Principle," from the *NYT* of June 15, 2003.[2] Quoting an Israeli political theorist, Yaron Ezrahi, he argues that only the United States, "an external force," can rescue the Israelis and Palestinians from their self-destructive war against each other. The United States of America is the "only reality principle." The United States alone can save the day "with its influence, its wisdom and, if necessary, its troops."

How illuminating is this?

Is the United States altogether "an external force" in its dealings with Israel? No American politician or media commentator can candidly examine this question without serious damage to his career. It is much safer to take the position that Israel is a client state of the United States, a strategic asset that polices America's friends and foes alike in the oil-rich Middle East. This is also the premise behind Friedman's description of the United States as the "only reality principle" in the conflict between Israel and the Palestinians.

The notion that Israel serves American interests in the Middle East is insupportable. At the least, it ignores three refractory facts. If indeed the United States acted in its own best interests *vis-à-vis* Israel, why would the American Israel Public Affairs Committee (AIPAC) exert itself so mightily to ensure that the US Presidency, Congress and media remain firmly committed to Israeli hegemony over its neighbors? In other words, why would American Jewry engage in such a monumentally wasteful exercise? Then, there is the curious fact that the United States was deeply concerned, during the

---

[2] Thomas Friedman, "The Reality Principle," *New York Times*, June 15, 2003, Section 4 , Page 13 , Column 1.

two Gulf Wars, to keep Israel *out* of these conflicts. If Israel were a strategic asset, would it not be helping the United States in these two wars? Third, on the rare occasions when a US President has opposed an official Israeli position, even when this was a mild rebuke, he has been forced to backtrack after running into massive opposition from both parties in the Congress. Who controls the Congress: the President or the Israeli lobby?

There are a few more glittering gems embedded in Mr. Friedman's column. Although Israel has the right to "pursue its mortal enemies, just as America does," he explains, it cannot "do it with reckless abandon." "America will never have to live with Mr. bin Laden's children. They are far away and always will be. Israel will have to live with the Palestinians, after the war. They are right next door and always will be." Now that should be illuminating to an America that was "changed for ever" by the events of 9-11, an America whose daily nightmare now is the looming threat of a chemical, biological or dirty-bomb attack on its home ground.

Next, consider Friedman's fears that the Palestinians are "capable only of self-destructive revenge, rather than constructive restraint and reconciliation." Again, how illuminating that Friedman should exclude Israelis from this anxious train of thought. There is amnesia here too. It is odd (or is it illuminating?) that *NYT*'s foreign affairs columnist forgets some pertinent history. The Palestinians demonstrated seven years of "constructive restraint and reconciliation" between 1993 and 2000, even as the Israelis – in clear violation of the Oslo Accord – continued their colonization of the West Bank, confiscating Palestinian lands, and building and expanding settlements that laid siege to Palestinian communities. In the end, what did the Palestinians get for relinquishing their historical right to 78 percent of historical Palestine? The Israelis made the now-notorious "generous offer" of Palestinian Bantustans. That is when the Palestinians, threatened with extinction, mounted their second Intifada.

Friedman asserts that on the Israeli side, only the "extremist Jewish settlers" oppose the two-state solution. In other words, all the other Israelis – the 'moderate' Jewish settlers and the Israelis settled inside the green line – support the two-state solution. Could it be that a small band of "extremist Jewish settlers" – these settlements did not crop up in one day – has imposed its extremist vision on the overwhelming majority of Israelis? How does that happen in the only democracy in the Middle East? Now, isn't that illuminating?

Is there a subliminal message in Friedman's discourse on "The Reality Principle?" I think there is one. It is contained in a single word – "troops." Only the United States, he claims, can save the day "with its influence, its wisdom and, if necessary, its *troops* (emphasis added)." Friedman is suggesting – of course, he is only suggesting – that "if necessary" the United States should take its war on "terrorism" to Gaza and the West Bank.

In 1993, the United States-cum-Israel chose Yasir Arafat and his "security services" to "discipline their own people." When Arafat "proved unwilling to do that consistently," Bush/Sharon replaced him with Mahmoud Abbas. It now appears that Abbas too may refuse to take his marching orders from Jerusalem or Washington. Of course, the Israelis could finish the job on their own, but it would be too dangerous. As Friedman puts it, "If Israelis try to do it, it [the cancer] will only metastasize." Friedman has a solution: give the job to American troops.

Twice a week Friedman delivers his perorations on the Arabs, Iran, Israel, Turkey, the Middle East and the Islamicate world more generally. In addition, over the years, as the *NYT*'s regular commentator on the Middle East, he has built a reputation as America's chief opinion-maker on the region. Does he deserve that reputation? Does he offer a balanced, objective, or *American* perspective on the region? Out of political correctness, most Americans will answer in the affirmative, but I have some nagging doubts.

In a recent television interview with Charlie Rose, Mr. Friedman said, "Israel was central to my life as it was to all my friends." He was reminiscing about his years in high school. "Today," he laments, "I'm probably the only one of my friends who is still emotionally involved in Israel."[3] Now, I would not have mentioned this if Friedman were not America's journalistic sage on Arabs and Muslims. However, since he is, I may be excused for thinking that this confession is pertinent to his sermons on the Middle East.

Isn't that illuminating?

---

3 "Friedman: Will Jews Still Care?" *Forward*, June 6, 2003: www.forward. com/issues/2003/03.06.06/news3b.html.

CHAPTER TWENTY

Lerner, Said and the Palestinians

"*… Allah is the best of plotters.*"

Qur'ān: 8:30

"*And every nation hath its term, and when its term cometh, they cannot put it off an hour nor yet advance it.*"

Qur'ān: 7:34

"*Every indigenous people will resist alien settlers as long as they see any hope of ridding themselves of the danger of foreign settlement. This is how the Arabs will behave and will go on behaving so long as they possess a gleam of hope that they can prevent 'Palestine' from becoming the land of Israel.*"

Ze'ev Jabotinsky (1923)[1]

June 18, 2003

Very few intellectuals in our times would measure up to Edward Said in the eulogies he received upon his death last year. Indirectly, every obituary, tribute, essay, reminiscence honoring his memory was a rebuke to the mercenaries who populate

[1] Ze'ev Jabotinsky, "The iron wall," *Rassvyet*, 4 November 1923: www. Marxists.de/ middleast/ironwall/ironwall.htm

our media, academia and that execrable category, think tanks. But would they notice?

Yet, I chanced upon one obituary notice that I found troubling. I was troubled because it was from Rabbi Michael Lerner who has risked the opprobrium of America's Jewish establishment by his opposition to the Israeli Occupation of the West Bank and Gaza.[2] At one time, he had to seek police protection in the face of death threats from pro-Israeli Americans.

It is not that the Rabbi does not praise Edward Said. He pays "tribute to a great thinker and writer whose contribution to contemporary intellectual life deserves our respect and appreciation." Said was a "powerful and passionate advocate for his *own* people, the Palestinians (emphasis added)." And that's all?

The Rabbi reserves his deepest respect, however, for the way in which Edward Said "publicly challenged Arafat and his *thuggish* ways (emphasis added)." Actually, challenging Arafat became a commonplace amongst Palestinians after he traded the rights of Palestinians for policing rights *over* Palestinians. The pointed reference to Arafat's "thuggish ways" is gratuitous. This phrase belongs to the lexicon of Zionist demonization of Palestinians.

Then come the accusations against Said. He did not "sympathize with the plight of European Jews and the way that their returning to the place they perceived to be their ancient homeland was not an act of Western colonialism." It is a circuitous sentence, a bit jumbled and problematic too.

Here is how I make sense of the Rabbi's syntax. First, he posits that the creation of Israel was not an "act of Western colonialism," something Edward Said knew or should have known. From this, the Rabbi infers that Said's opposition to Zionism was due to his lack of

---

[2] Michael Lerner, "Edward Said," *Tikkun*, November/December 2003.

sympathy for (a) the "plight of European Jews" and (b) their right to return to "the place they perceived to be their ancient homeland."

The first charge is scandalous. Only someone seized with anti-Semitic loathing could lack "sympathy" for the centuries of suffering endured by European Jews. Unwittingly, therefore, the Rabbi accuses Said of anti-Semitism, which I am sure the Rabbi will promptly disavow. Or, is the Rabbi saying that European Jews had earned the right – because of their long suffering – to a Jewish state in Palestine, even if this would lead to the destruction of Palestinian society. Said's sin, then, is that he does not recognize *this* Jewish 'right.' Against this charge, the world will acquit Edward Said. The Rabbi will agree that self-destructive sympathy does not come naturally to most people.

The second charge stems from the premise of a Jewish right of return. In this case, we are asked to concede that the "perception" that Palestine is "their ancient homeland" gives European Jews the right to return. And this right is comprehensive. It empowers European Jews to 'repossess' Palestine – take it away from the Palestinians – in order to establish a state *of* the Jewish people.

The Jewish right of return claims legitimacy by appeals to its ancient nationalist mythology. No system of law elevates a perceived claim, by an individual or group, into a legally enforceable right. Nor does any system of law confer on any people a perpetual right to a country they once inhabited (or may have inhabited), much less one they left (or claim to have left) some eighteen hundred years ago. In effect, then, the Rabbi faults Said for not accepting Jewish mythology as the law for the Palestinians.

Rabbi Lerner also accuses the Palestinians – and Said, by association – of immorality. "He never took the step of acknowledging that Palestinian resistance to Jewish immigration in the years when

Jews were trying to escape the gas chambers of Europe or the displaced persons camps of 1945-48 was immoral." At best, the argument is tendentious.

Is the Rabbi conceding – perhaps unwittingly – that Palestinian resistance to Jewish immigration was moral *before* Hitler opened the gas chambers? Was it moral then because Jews were entering Palestine under a Zionist plan – first conceived in 1897 and ratified by Britain in 1917 – whose goal was to create a Jewish state that would dispossess the Palestinians. This organized Jewish immigration amounted to a Jewish invasion that would necessarily lead to the displacement and dispossession of Palestinians.

Should the Palestinians have ceased their resistance because Nazi persecution of Jews in Europe – by accelerating Jewish immigration into Palestine – was bringing their own demise nearer, and making it more certain? Did the Zionists at this time start a dialogue with the Palestinians, explaining to them that the Jews escaping Nazi persecution would enter only as refugees, seeking temporary shelter in Palestine before they could be relocated to countries where they would be welcome? Indeed, Nazi persecution became the perverse – if unintended – engine for completing the Zionist project. Should it then have mattered to the Palestinians that the Jewish immigrants who would accelerate their dispossession were fleeing persecution?

There is another flaw in the Rabbi's train of thought. He assumes that Palestine was the only destination for Jewish refugees escaping Nazi persecution. On the face of it, it sounds implausible that none of the Allied countries, whose war effort could have been greatly aided by the influx of Jewish skills, expertise and capital, would have offered refuge, permanent or temporary, to the Jews fleeing Nazi Europe.

In support of this assumption, the Zionists point to the resistance to Jewish immigration in the United States. But this won't wash. One has to ask if the world Jewish hierarchy, by now fully committed to the creation of Israel, had a real interest in exerting its power to overcome American opposition to Jewish immigration? If the Jewish lobbies in the United States could offset the State Department's opposition to the creation of Israel, were they not capable of overcoming the Administration's resistance to Jewish immigration? Moreover, the United States was not the only feasible destination for Jewish refugees.

Rabbi Lerner's difficulties have their source in the deep contradictions of Zionism. This was a nationalist project unlike any other because the people – European Jews – it defined as a nation did not possess the territorial attributes of a nation; they did not constitute a majority in any of the territories that they inhabited. In fact, they were everywhere a small minority. It was imperative for this nationalist project, therefore, to acquire a territory where it could exercise the collective rights of nationhood, viz. sovereignty and statehood.

The founders of the Zionist project knew instinctively that it would be impractical – indeed suicidal – to try to acquire territory for a Jewish state within Europe. Instead, they decided that they would harness the support of European powers to create the territorial basis of their state *outside* of Europe. Britain was the first great power to sponsor the Zionist project.

Palestine offered the ideal location. Its historical value – as the site of the ancient Jewish state and the land promised by Yahweh to the Hebrews – would be useful in mobilizing Jewish support for the Zionist project. Since it was not yet a European colony, it would be easier to persuade a European power to help create a Jewish state in Palestine, serving as a "rampart of Europe against Asia, an outpost of civilization against barbarism."[3] Palestine contained Christian holy

---

3 Theodore Herzl, *The Jewish state* (1896): www.geocities.com/Vienna/6640 /zion/

lands too, and this was another incentive for Europeans to take it away from the Muslims and give it to the Jews, a Biblical people. Finally, the project would realize the anti-Semite's dream of cleansing Christian Europe of its Jewish population.

Inevitably, since its inception, the Zionist project had two defining features. It was an imperialist project – a form of surrogate imperialism – since Britain, the leading imperialist power, would acquire Palestine in fulfillment of a deal with an influential segment of the Jewish bourgeoisie. Necessarily, it was also a colonial-settler project, since it sought to create a state *of* European Jews *on* Palestinian land. This would entail, in some combination, the displacement and marginalization of the Palestinians.

These are the "wrongs" that the Zionists regard as right, as legitimate, as moral, as necessary for Jewish survival, for Jewish power. Rabbi Lerner is a committed Zionist. He makes no bones about that. Though an American himself, he informs us – without comment – that his son had served with the Israeli Occupation Army in the West Bank.[4] As a Zionist, the Rabbi accuses the Palestinians – and Edward Said – of failing to acknowledge the wrongs done to them as right, as moral, as necessary.

Of course, Rabbi Lerner has more heart than most Zionists. He concedes that the Palestinians too have "rights" to Palestine, the same as the Jews. He concedes this *because* you cannot be a pro-Israeli without conceding these rights: because there can be no prospect of Jewish security without mollifying the Palestinians. The "equal" rights he grants the Palestinians, however, only allows them a "state" on 22 percent of historic Palestine. He does not contemplate any Palestinian right of return. No "equality" there.

---

4 Rabbi Michael Lerner, "It's time to atone when we see only our own pain," *Los Angeles Times*, October 13, 2000.

The creation of Israel was a power play. It was born out of the contradictions of the history of European Jews, a contradiction that would be resolved by the confluence of Jewish influence and Western imperial power, combining to serve the interests of both. The cost of this project to Palestinians, to Arabs, to Muslims, was not even an issue in an era dominated by Western racism and bigotry – of the Christian, Jewish and secular variety.

As the contradictions of the Zionist project deepen, forcing it to draw the United States directly into the conflict, that same racism and bigotry are being mobilized in the West, and especially the United States, to support another assault on the rights of the Palestinians, Arabs and Muslims. Slowly, reflexively, a segment of the Muslim population, a small segment still I believe, is being energized to take back their lands, their dignity and rights, their place under the sun. Some of them are even imitating the bloody-mindedness of their foes.

Is this the clash of civilizations between the West and the Islamicate world expected by Samuel Huntington? Was this conflict inevitable given the confluence of four factors: the dependency of US economy on Middle Eastern oil; the insertion of Israel in the Arab heartland; the advanced Israelization of the United States, a consequence of the Zionist project; and an Islamicate world, a large segment of the Periphery, beaten in the nineteenth century, divided, humiliated, expropriated, now reaching a quarter of the world's population, and struggling to regain its rights, its autonomy, its dignity, its splintered wholeness?

Are Islamicate societies seeking to reconstitute their life on the primordial foundations – lost in the stress of modernization – of a perennial encounter "between God as such and man as such," between the transcendent, creative principle of the universe and a theomorphic man endowed with intellect, free will and speech?[5] Alternatively, are these societies today what their adversaries say they are – raging over their loss of power, over being left behind by the West? Did they 'fail' to modernize because of flaws in the 'deep structure' of their culture; and are they now seeking, out of spite, to destroy the leader of the modern, democratic and powerful West?

We cannot tell where this contest – at bottom, an economic contest – will take us. It may end quickly, producing a 'thousand years' of US-Israeli hegemony over the Islamicate world; or it may lead to the decline of American power in that region. If it is the latter, it may restore a balance between the West and Islamdom, an equilibrium shattered in the nineteenth century. However, these options are simplistic. History may hold surprises, as it often does, especially for those who think they have the power to make things happen according to well-laid plans. The unintended consequences have a habit of making *things* a bit messier. The two American victories – over Nazis and the Soviets – do not translate into an ineluctable law of invincibility. The Islamicate peoples are not defending outmoded systems or some unnatural tyranny. They are defending something more basic: their lives, their livelihood and the way they want to live.

---

[5] Frithjof Schuon, *Understanding Islam* (Bloomington, IN: World Wisdom Books, 1994): 1.

Index of Names

Index of Subjects